Ears of Corn

Ears of Corn

P. C. Mullen

WIPF & STOCK · Eugene, Oregon

EARS OF CORN

Copyright © 2019 Philip Christopher Mullen. All rights reserved. Except for brief quotations in critical publications or reviews, no part of this book may be reproduced in any manner without prior written permission from the publisher. Write: Permissions, Wipf and Stock Publishers, 199 W. 8th Ave., Suite 3, Eugene, OR 97401.

Wipf & Stock
An Imprint of Wipf and Stock Publishers
199 W. 8th Ave., Suite 3
Eugene, OR 97401

www.wipfandstock.com

PAPERBACK ISBN: 978-1-5326-8376-3
HARDCOVER ISBN: 978-1-5326-8377-0
EBOOK ISBN: 978-1-5326-8378-7

Manufactured in the U.S.A.   SEPTEMBER 23, 2019

Scripture quotations taken from the New Revised Standard Version Bible, copyright © 1989 National Council of the Churches of Christ in the United States of America. Used by permission. All rights reserved worldwide.

These Ears of Corn

Gathered and rubbed in my hands

Upon broken Sabbaths,

I offer first to my Wife,

And then to my other Friends.

George MacDonald,
Dedication in Unspoken Sermons, Vol I

Contents

Preface ✦ ix

1. You Search the Scriptures ✦ 1
2. Why Judge Ye Not? ✦ 13
3. A Stranger They Will Not ✦ 25
4. The Reflection ✦ 39
5. One God, the Father ✦ 48
6. As Sin Came into the World ✦ 61
7. For They Know Not ✦ 76
8. Was It Not Necessary? ✦ 93
9. He Had Compassion ✦ 109
10. Boasting in Our Hope ✦ 118
11. To Reconcile All Things ✦ 129
12. Keep Awake ✦ 146

Preface

ONE WRITES A BOOK for the same reason that one reads one: to find God. Doubtless there are many who disagree. They believe that books exist for finding things other than God, things like beauty, joy, escape, truth. I ask, what are these but shadows of our God? Is not every question mark a hidden longing after God, every exclamation point a joyful cry of his praise? Is not every sentence a meditation on the mystery that God is forever creating, and every word an attempt to lay hold of one of his thoughts?

We are all, every day, writing our own book, and gathering our ears of corn, trying to find our God. Here is my gathering in written form. I dedicate it first to my wife, Nicole, and then, as my forefather in the faith said years ago, to my other friends.

I

You Search the Scriptures

"You search the scriptures, because you think that in them
you have eternal life; and it is they that testify on my behalf.
Yet you refuse to come to me to have life."

JOHN 5:39, 40

WHY DO YOU SEARCH the Scriptures? Why else but to know truth? But then, truth must be the final end towards which the searching of the Scriptures labors. All tools we use, all arguments, all authorities and commentaries, yea, all thinking itself, exist for the sake of attaining the pure and simple truth, to have it dwell in our hearts and rule our spirits, and so make us true. How easily the mind is distracted from this goal! How easily we turn from journeying towards the Land of Truth itself, to rest content in the cave of *what-someone-thought-was-true!* How could we ever be satisfied with such, if we were true lovers of the truth?

What good is it to know what another thinks of truth? Compared to knowing truth itself, it is a trifle—a mere historicism—a question of infinitely secondary importance. Why then do we labor to prove what this or that thinker thought true? No doubt because we love the fellow seeker, this forefather of wisdom who has led our soul by the hand on its own journey towards the homeland. But for all this, our love for our fellow ought never to replace our love for truth. The more noble-minded and pure-hearted the one whose thought we study, the more surely would that one cast aside all false opinion and beclouded conclusion to lay hold of the truth. Would not St. Paul himself, if he were shown some obscurity in his argument or some erroneous deduction that could be made from his words, upon being told by a fellow seeker of truth and follower of Jesus Christ, would not St. Paul, I say, join hands with his opponent and seek to purify his own understanding, his own appreciation, his own reasons for believing in God's sweet truth? And if Paul would not, would he be a true heart seeking truth above all else, in all its profundity and loveliness?

We use other's thoughts best, not when we adopt them thoughtlessly, worse still when we defend them blindly, but when, feeling them true, we assimilate them into our own true-knowing, and look at the world through a newly forged vision.

"Do you then put yourself on the same authority as Paul? As Christ himself? Is there no room for you to bow your mind to truths too high for you to comprehend? Are you saying that unless you can comprehend it, a thing cannot be true?"

I ask, if one cannot see a truth, how can it appear to him true? And if it does not appear true, how then can he bow to it in honest submission? Surely, the one who does not know the nature of the thing he is bowing to cannot bow to it in good conscience, not to say rational mind. If you insist that he bows anyway, not understanding why, I ask, where is the good in a bow made blindly?

If one cannot see the truth in a thing, he cannot believe it true—unless, that is, he lies to himself. But then he sins, against both himself and his God. Did not Paul warn against such when he charged Timothy: wage the good warfare, holding faith *and a good conscience*? Why a good conscience? He tells us: "Because by rejecting it, some have made shipwreck of their faith."[1] Shipwreck of faith! By denying conscience! Friend, how backward that theology is, stuck in the crusted pages of history, which supposes conscience has no place in growing faith, and plays no part in free inquiry! How wrong they are who hold it is a voice to be muted when it cries against tradition! To shut out conscience is to shut out the Spirit of God. The one who rejects conscience damages what little faith he has—or is beginning to have—and goes to make it a poor, weak, low thing. His faith is kept alive, if all, only by fear. It sits caged in his soul, starving and crouched and afraid, like a beast abused. How far this faith is from that strong and healthy faith, fed by the nourishing power of the Living One! Faith can only be strong to the degree that conscience is alive and working and constantly responsive

---

1. 1 Tim 1:19

to every truth that comes spontaneously into the mind. Insofar as one is bound to have faith in God therefore, he is bound to follow conscience and to assent to nothing which seems to him false or unworthy of belief, nor believe a thing merely out of fear.

But this is very different from saying that all that one may believe is that which he can comprehend. God shall no one ever comprehend. But the soul shall one day find rest, yea, even joy, in this incomprehension. In the highest union of the soul with God, the fact that the divine beauty far surpasses even the unspeakable loveliness that the soul is bathed in, the very fact that God is still infinitely *more*, must itself cause the soul a unique rapturous delight. The ineffable grandeur could not but fill creatures united to it with a bliss unspeakable. But this incomprehension is very different from the incomprehension attending the submission of one's intellect to what one cannot see as true. Such an incomprehension comes, not *simply* because one cannot see a thing as true, but because he sees it as untrue. In the first case, the incomprehensibility is set before the mind to gaze and wonder at: a mystery, a sphere with no beginning, a space with no boundary, a never-ending stream of ever flowing life. In the second, what confronts it is a contradiction, a clashing of assertions, two opposite poles vying for sameness. The mind does not breathe in mystery, but chokes on impossibility. The mutual incompatibility that it meets is a shrieking, irreconcilable unthinkable. It is not that the thing *may be*, but is too grand to appreciate. It is that it *cannot* be and conveys no meaning at all.

"You then set yourself up over Christ."

I set myself alongside Christ—or rather, my understanding of him. I know well—and sorrowfully—that I cannot ask Christ my questions and audibly hear his reply. Alas, I cannot look in his face as his disciples did, and watch it live and move as he answers me! But, friend, I can imagine myself doing so. I can picture me asking and him looking and responding. Knowing this I ask, do you imagine Christ would be angry with me for wanting to ask a thing that lies on my heart?

Christ would either answer my questions, or rebuke me. If he answered them, I would be the better, assuming I understood him, which, if I did not, I would, I hope, continue to ask more until I did. For what good is asking a question, if no more understanding follows? On the other hand, if Christ rebuked me, this would be either for my benefit and to deepen my understanding, or it would not. If it would not, Christ cannot be a lover of those who seek truth. For his aim in answering questions is not to increase understanding. How then could he be the Truth, since the truth is

Ears of Corn

that which dispels ignorance from darkened minds? If Christ will not grant answers to one who asks, not in arrogant pride, but in tearful and hungry humility, can he be the one who tells his followers to ask so that it may be given, to seek so that they will find? Is this seeking not the very thing which he tells us will set us free? Yet how can we be freed, if we are barred from seeking? How shall the door be opened, if we are told we cannot knock? Could Christ mean what he said, if he were angry with you and me, friend, for asking our questions, whatever they be, so long as they are asked in honest humility?

Do you think that there is any *possible* thought, any question—any spiritual *quest* of human soul that would be too small, too insignificant to the heart of Jesus Christ? I cannot believe such of the Savior. For verily, he came to save the soul entire, questions and longings and fears and all.

Then again, if Christ would indeed rebuke me, and if the rebuke was indeed for my benefit, are we not still left with the same?—that in any case, it is better for the thirsting soul to bring its questions to its Lord and God? Therefore I say, lay bare the questions that burn in thy bosom. The sooner we are rebuked by the master, the better!

Let me then ask again. What purpose is there in studying theology or church history? What purpose is there in reading commentaries or in memorizing Scripture? What good is it to ponder over the words of Jesus or know the system of this or that thinker or recite the creeds? Again I answer. These things exist to serve a unified and mighty end: so that we may know the truth. But are we to know truth simply for truth's sake? No. We are to know it for the sake of becoming true. We are to know it so to become altogether strong, lovely, good, and pure children of God.

Have you ever thought, friend, that the whole purpose for us in knowing Jesus, is so that we could become true, beautiful, and good human beings? The main purpose for our knowing him is not so that we could *merely* quote his words. A parrot could do that. Rather, it is so that we can become *like* him. Knowing his words is but a means to this great end. In this respect—and mind what I say closely—*in this respect,* it does not even matter if we know what Christ said. The village girl who never heard of Jesus but forgave her school mate for teasing her has the spirit of Christ working in her young heart, though she has never heard of the New Testament or the one who saved his people from their sins.

I believe that the whole race needs Jesus Christ, and that all are saved through his obedient act of perfected humanity. But suppose that Christ could look upon another world of human beings. Suppose he could see in such a world a true man, a good woman, an absolutely pure human being. I ask, would it bother Jesus if the one he saw had never known that a man named Jesus Christ had lived? Would Christ himself not rejoice simply in the goodness of the human being, in the fact that such a one *was* and was a noble son or daughter of God? Would he not be unspeakably glad in the perfect Childhood of his Father that had blossomed into the mighty spring radiance that was that person's soul? I do not say that anyone can be good without Christ working in him. I take that to be a metaphysical impossibility. But it is not difficult to believe—is it not impossible to doubt?—that Christ can work in one without that one knowing it. Or do you not think that the Spirit of Christ, that is, the Spirit of truest humanity born out of the imagination of the living God, is working in you all the time, even when you know it not? Indeed, it may be working most when you know it least!

If you are a Christian who believes in a God of love, how could you ever think you were in anything other than a universe bathed in a divine energy unspeakably tender, omnipotently fierce, unfathomably interpenetrating, working in you every moment? Long before the dawn of what you call yourself peeped over the brim of your outlooking soul, the spirit of Christ was working in you. What moves the embryo in the womb, what knits together its limbs and body, what draws the form that is there taking shape, mingling with matter—what directs all these things, if not almighty God, the ultimate Power and Love, working through and with the essentially human? Before you uttered your first word, before you thought your first thought, before your heart beat its first beat while you slumbered in the forethought of the universe, the spirit of God was already working in you, friend. The Divine Maker was already, with his invisible and love-driven hands, molding the depths of thy deepest self, through the eternal firstborn, Jesus Christ.

Yet how are we to know Christ? I said we ought to ask him our questions. But how? We cannot speak to him. We cannot audibly hear his voice. We do not even have words that he has written down. And, though we do have words written by those who knew him, even those people very often misunderstood him. Is it not therefore likely that *we* shall misunderstand *them*?

Let us ask: would not Jesus, if his goal was to bring men and women to a truer and better understanding of their relation to their Maker, would he not therefore of necessity talk at the level of his hearers? To teach one, that one must be met where he is. Accommodation must be made. Yet a student's mind must be stretched, not broken. To anyone who doubts that this was the way of Christ, or to one who doubts that such a thing occurs in the revelation between God and man, I ask him to honestly and diligently compare the Synoptics to the Gospel of John. I do not say that they contradict each another. But it cannot be doubted that in John we find a deepening of the revelation of the Son than what is found in the Synoptics. Yet a deeper revelation calls for a deeper soul to hold that revelation; a heart cannot hold what is has no room to contain.. Therefore did not the writer of John in some sense better receive the truths that Jesus taught—thus better incorporate them into himself—than the other writers?

"You cast doubt upon the inspiration of the Bible!"

I do not grant it. But what does it matter if I did? How can the casting of doubt ever *trouble* us, friends? We seek truth, do we not? What would it matter if in the whole world not a soul knew or had ever heard of the Bible, if the whole world were nothing but good and true and pure children of God? We must never forget that the Bible exists, as does the New Testament, as do the writings of Paul and Peter and James and John, as do the words—yea the very deeds—of Christ himself, not to equip us with arguments for arguments sake, still less to make us creatures of rote. They exist to make us like Jesus. That is, to make us into perfectly good, true, lovely human beings, fashioned into full brothers and sisters of humanity, fully devoted to our God.

But again, how does one become such a thing? How does one know what such a thing looks like, opened up and living in the world? We must be our very best selves, must become better than what we fear we cannot be, by being full children of our Father like Jesus. But how to do it? If we are to be like Christ, what does that mean? How do we know him, so that we can be like him? What we have of him written in the New Testament shows us much of him. But is there no closer we can press into him to know him better?

The one who loves the words of Jesus in the New Testament best will want most more than those words alone. For he knows that the letter exists for the Spirit, never the Spirit for the letter. He understands why Christ said that the Sabbath was made for man, not man for the Sabbath. To the one who would rule his life by the text alone, and who claims to go not one atom beyond its words, his individual life—yea his whole thinking and doing and being in the world—must be an enigma, a thing unspeakable. How could one take a single step if he supposed his every action must, before he could do or think it, be found in the New Testament, as either commanded or permitted? Where would be his faith?

What we want, friends, and what the soul yearns for with unutterable longing, is to know not merely the *words* of Jesus, but to know the *man* himself. We want not the *record* of him, but *him*. What does it matter if we knew the very words that came forth from his lips—yea, if we sat at his feet night and day and heard the very tone and richness of his voice—if we did not know his person? We want to push past the appearance—which is merely the man as he *seems* through the matter he uses to convey himself—and enter into communion with the very heart-soul..

Who does not long for such a union with every soul he loves? Who is not dissatisfied with the fact that he must always be separated from, since not in absolute union with, his friends, his family, his lover? How often I have looked into the eyes of another and felt them so marvelous, so unique, so full of something within! For good reason did the ancients call them portals of the soul! For do they not speak to us of the deeper thing: the *person* that they hide? How naturally to believe that, when we look into another's eyes, those eyes show us, not merely a concourse of atoms moving in a void, but, somehow, *someone*! Who has ever loved that does not wish to push deeper into those eyes, as beautiful as they are, to lay hold of and intermix with the spirit inside? I imagine such a union ineffable, a mutual indwelling so interpenetrating and fulfilling and overflowing with loving warmth, as the very joy of heaven itself.

And yet, if the eyes show us something of someone which his words do not and indeed cannot show us, how can we be satisfied in our knowing of Christ, if our only way of knowing him lay in the reading of the *words* of the New Testament? Mark, I do not say such reading does not show us the Lord. It does indeed. But I do say it cannot show us all that can be known of him, all that the yearning heart wants and therefore *must* know of him.

How then are we to know Christ in the deep way that we wish? I know no other way save one. It is a way you have been doing all your life, a way you do every day, indeed every time you have ever thought of Christ, or, for that matter, anyone at all. We must know Jesus Christ by *imagining* him.

"What! By imagining him? What then is preventing me from making up my own version of him and doing what I please?"

Friend, have you not—have all people not—been imagining him from the beginning? One cannot think about, cannot interpret, cannot know the personality of any person at all without using one's imagination. You have surely read books about Christ, heard sermons on him, and thought a great deal about what he said and what he meant when he spoke. What is this but you using your imagination to get at the man? Why, you do not even know what his face looked like! Every picture you have of him is a product more or less of your own construction, is it not? But has that prevented you from knowing him? Christ, you know, spoke in parables. What is a parable, but the setting before the imagination some situation in which it goes on to draw some conclusion, some deeper truth? Tell me you wish to know the spirit of someone without using your imagination, and I will tell you it cannot be done. Take away imagination, and you take away thought itself. What meaning can the mind abstract without running on the fuel of the *imagination*? No doubt there is great danger that lies in imagining the spirit and message of Christ. But that danger is present from the fact that we are not ourselves perfectly good and true and lovely people, not because when we try to know Jesus, we do so the only way it is possible to know anyone.

To know the man Jesus Christ, we must imagine him. But how? By taking what we already know of goodness, love, compassion and truth and applying it in our here and now. To ask, "What would Jesus do?" is the same as to ask, "What would the idealized human, the most true, good, and loving one working in me do? If Jesus Christ could take my soul and fashion it into its grandest potential, if he could put his spirit into my spirit and so create a strong and true and unique child of God—my best me—how would I be?" Thus the image of the perfect which we must model ourselves by and strive to attain is one discovered by continually imagining and asking our Ideal Christ to remake us into our better humanity.

Christ is at once both himself and our best self speaking to us, thereby calling us deeper into both himself and our self. Christ is the Christ—the Divine Humanity—because he is Divine Humanity producing an image of your best self, which you then strive to be. This is how Christ saves: by being born—by becoming flesh—in our self. He is our best self only insofar as he is himself—the Son of God—worked out in us, coming alive. This is the fruit of the Incarnation: the idealization of innumerable souls, the raising of the human, the ever-expanding of the creature into its greatest possible, and altogether unique and unrepeatable, self. Our best self is Jesus Christ in us, and Jesus Christ in us is our salvation.

To the degree that the letter of the Bible leads us deeper into our essential humanity and therefore brotherhood with Christ, it serves its divine, life-giving purpose. To the degree it leads away from this, it brings forth death. We must do the best we can with what we already know and have, incorporating such into our wrestle-reading of the Scripture. This is necessarily different from taking a given passage of the Bible, which, taken at face value, contradicts notions we know to be good and true, and submitting to the passage, therefore abandoning what we already know and have. For what we already know and have is nothing else than our true humanity, our true Christ-self alive and working in us, giving birth to our true individuality and our own Divine Childhood. This voice in our heart, this *conscience*—this our being *with-knowledge*—is the only is the only real contact we have made with the Good and True. All else is an impression, made by another. Thus to abandon the voice we hear would be to doom ourselves to a universe where we could never ourselves touch the Good and True, where we could never trust our own hearts. We could then never set about becoming more than what we were, by being more truly what we know we should be.

"But does not such a principle reduce to a vague generality? The very task is to know the *man*, and yet, by following this path of idealized imagining, we shall not know the man at all, but only our imagined version of him."

I say, if Jesus Christ really is from the Father, and really is an infinitely true human being, then, since we too are human beings, he must be like us, and we must be like him. How therefore can we know him without knowing ourselves? To know Christ, then, is to know oneself, and to know of oneself what one could be, for in knowing this, one knows the potential of his own humanity. Christ is the potential of humanity realized. To know him we must know the essentially human, and to know this, we must know who we are and who we must become.

How then are we to become more and more like Jesus? How therefore but to ask the essentially human to come deeper into us and make us more like itself? For us to be fully human is to fully imitate Jesus, for humanity itself is the condition of an emerging, evermore dependent, conscious relation to its God. At present, although Christ is in all people, all people are not yet fully awake to this relation. We must have faith that they will be one day—for do they not come from the same Father as we? In the meantime we must grow in Christ more and more, until we too share his consciously radiant closeness to the Living One, the Great Parent of us all.

"You teach a strange, not to say dangerous doctrine. Be yourself and be truly human? With this teaching, cannot one do anything he wants? Be a murderer, a thief, a slanderer, a self-centered and violent egoist? Why not be an atheist and deny all meaning to the universe and humanity? You offer us no protection from what is evil in ourselves! You offer us no protection from our fallen nature! Do you not know the inherent wickedness of humanity?"

What can save humanity but that humans become fully true human beings and altogether good children of God? The *protection* from our fallen nature comes from the *perfection* of our current one. Christ was fully man. Thus it is not the humanity itself which is evil. It is the fear and selfishness and meanness that plague it. In God's great universe, can a thing be fully itself without also being fully good, fully beautiful, fully lovely, fully true? It cannot be, else God made that which finds its fulfillment in its own warped nature. In God's universe, for a thing to grow most truly into itself is for it to reach its divinely appointed beatitude.

Christ is the eternal humanity, which is born in each human heart and blooms into life through God. Our highest calling and deepest purpose is to allow this eternal humanity to become fully alive in us, to merge into one with our being. Who is Jesus Christ? Himself—a flowering humanity, an emerging and expanding and endlessly growing God-consciousness of human soul. The historical man stands as but a peg to hang this grand mystery on, this all encompassing Myth, this interpreting of reality. Christ is not a single instance, located in the frozen past, but an ever present, indwelling person—a Thou—who we call to to bring us into our own deepest, truest humanity.

What is it to be fully human? It is to have a cosmic, undefeatable faith in the Living One. It is to trust in God the Father and draw strength from his Son, our elder brother, Jesus, who taught us that our humanity is perfected when we believe that there is an all-relating, absolutely beautiful, and inexorable God. It is to believe that this all-Father created each human being and thereby knit humanity together as a single creature, a united organism, such that every piece is necessarily related to every other. This truth— the absolute Fatherhood of God over all that is—is the greatest message of the Christ. It is the electricity that makes his heart beat and the atmosphere which saturates his spirit. It is the foundation on which his soul stands; the pillow he lays his head upon at night; the morning sun which enlightens his eyes every day. The Great Paternity of God is Jesus Christ's meaning. It is his reason for being. To live in a universe made by his Father, and to live among his fellow brothers and sisters and to love them—it may be with a love fierce and hard—this must be the way of things, the only way of true humanity. He shall live no other way. If we are to know Jesus, follow him, and spend our hearts and imaginations in understanding him, we can live no other way either.

Thus if we would be imitators of Christ, we must first believe that the world ought to be looked at as the offspring of One who loves all infinitely and higher and deeper than we can ever imagine; the One who loves such because he is what he is in his very relating to us as such a love. And we must believe that the real and most pure relation of the human soul to this One is childhood.

From the interconnectedness of our race and its unity in Jesus Christ, we must love our neighbors as ourselves. To truly love another as oneself is to recognize that every person is in us and that we are in every person. This is so—it *must* be so—because we all share a fundamental humanity. We are thus brought to our perfection by our entering into our fellow brothers and sisters so deeply that we consider them as our very self. We must break down the wall of separation, the wall of self-defense, the wall of thinking it impossible for there to be anything in common between us and our fellow human beings, in whatever condition they seem. We must go into our neighbor's heart, mind, and feeling. We must get into his very *person* and feel him as our own self, for we must love him as our self. What is more precious to a soul than itself? How therefore love another self, without looking at that self as if it were you? Do you not know, friend, that your neighbor is herself as much as you are yourself? She has a self, just like you. Therefore you are not that different. Our neighbor's moods, her thoughts, her failures: these must become ours, and we must think of them as if they really *were* ours. This does not mean we ought never to deal harshly with them; for very often we deal harshly with ourselves, and this justly. But how often do we thus *enter* another? How often do we allow our neighbor's feelings to become *our* feelings? Let us both hold the question-mirror up and say what we see.

Our essential connection to our neighbor cannot be otherwise, for we are all human beings. We must then strive for our compassion—our *entering into*—to reign so in our hearts that there becomes no human living—no human that ever lived, or will—that we look upon indifferently. It matters not how far away they are, how different their life may be, how foreign their feelings, fears, or beliefs, how apparently holy, how evidently wicked. No one is an island. So long as there is in front of me a *person*—no matter how *other* they may seem, no matter how twisted they may have become—she and I share the same birth of desire, the same fundamental consciousness, the same range of emotions, the same forms of experience, the same hopes, the same fears, the same orientation towards the good. Nor is that all, or least! In our souls we share the same image of God, and in our spirit the same Jesus Christ binds us all into one, in a way too deep for words or thought.

All other things Christ said and did must be interpreted in the light of these two truths: the eternal and all-relating Paternity that gives us being, and the eternal, divine brother and sisterhood of all humanity. The first gives rise to a horizon of infinite optimism, though it may take, at times, an adamantine will to keep in one's sights. The second declares an indissoluble bond between all human beings. On these two truths hang all the law and the prophets.

Or else, there is some greater message, some deeper undercurrent, that could underlie Jesus' teachings and stand behind them and give them life. To this source then we must turn, Christ himself being but the pointer to it and the messenger of it, rather than the divine thing itself, worked out in human form. Yet I ask, what could be greater than the universal Parenthood of God and the universal brotherhood of humanity, rooted in and interpenetrated by the Ideal Son? This just *is* the ultimate thought explaining our existence and pointing us with hope and faith to our glorious future. All other philosophies and teachings, being lesser truths, are enveloped by this great truth. Let us therefore set aside all lesser truths and man-made systems and listen to the Son of the Uncreated Truth, who asks, "Why do you not judge for yourselves what is right?"

2

Why Judge Ye Not?

"And why do you not judge for yourselves what is right?"
LUKE 12:57

IT IS EASY, WHEN reading the words of Jesus, to pass over some sentence of his which is couched in a larger context, and therefore to fail to see some great truth. We are eager to get to the heart of his meaning, the kernel of truth, and, from our earnestness, we do not let our eyes rest and our hearts dwell on absolutely all that he says. We would do well to remember the words of the Canaanite woman: even the crumbs can be eaten, if they fall from the master's table.

This problem of not seeing Jesus' words is compounded by the fact that, in many Bible translations, we have imposed on us inserted paragraph breaks and summary headings, as well as superscripts and footnotes and commentaries. Such things often prevent us from dwelling on the words of the text itself, and thus fix our thought on the unessential.

When meditating on the words of Jesus, as well as those of the Epistles, it is of benefit to remember four things. First, our Lord likely spoke native Aramaic, probably of a Galilean dialect, not English or even Greek. Second, the Greek of the original accounts is already both a language and a country removed from Christ the historical man himself. Third, when the texts were written, many years had passed since Christ walked the earth, and it is not impossible that some who lived after his death could have missapprehended or misstated his teachings or beliefs, in either word or writing. And fourth, in the original text, there is no punctuation. That is, there are no periods or commas, nor are there phrases and sentences which neatly interchange with our English phrases and sentences and their theologically loaded implications. The more one spends time with the Greek of the New Testament, the more one sees this third point especially.

Allow me to present an example. Below I present one passage, rendered in two ways. In the first case, I present a sentence as it reads from a common translation of the English Bible. In the second, the same sentence as it reads as a transliteration of the Greek. The passage is Mark 14:21.

1. For the Son of Man goes as it is written of him, but woe to that one by whom the Son of Man is betrayed. It would have been better for that one if he had not been born.

2. For indeed Son of Man goes as it has been written concerning him woe however to the man that by whom the Son of Man is betrayed good for him if had never been born the man that.

Do you see the possible difference in meaning here? In the first rendition, the structure of the sentence implies that it were better for the one who *betrayed* the Son of Man never to have been born. In the second rendition, however, it is more naturally seen as being good for *the Son of Man*—who is the *him* in the sentence—had not the betrayer been born. Thus, here is a case which, by the mere movement of words and the placing of commas, we arrive at a completely different meaning of the text of the New Testament, nay, even of the words of Jesus Christ. And a more monumental difference in implication can hardly be imagined! For the first rendition can be read, as fit in with its earlier context, as suggesting that Judas was predestined to do that which brought upon him a fate so terrible it would be better if he had never been born. This one thought is enough to undo all theology and all possible hope in God. For does it not imply that it would have been better if God had never created him? Perhaps not for our sake, you may think. But surely for Judas'!

Taking the first reading as true, we set up an infinite gulf between the will of the Son and the will of the Father. For the will of the Son may be *for* humanity, while the will of the Father, since he has predestined at least some for destruction, may be *against*. The Father may will damnation for some, while the Son may will salvation for all. Christ died for the whole world, yet the Father extends his hand to but a portion. But if we take the second rendition of the passage, the problem evaporates. It allows Christ's heart to be at one with the Father's, since neither would dream of creating any human being simply to torture it—or "permit" it to be tortured, for the wording comes to the same—for eternity. See how wild a thing our theology can become by the mere movement of words, by the slightest shift in letters! See how quickly our God can change from Jehovah into Molech! Did not the serpent deceive the race with one word? And did he not quote very God himself in doing so? Who then can deny that we ought to use the utmost care—even caution—when reading the words of Christ, as they have come to us down from the hands of translators, filtered through the minds of others? Especially when they present to us a God who seems evil!

Verily we get closer to the heart of Christ, friends, in the second reading of the verse in Mark. For it is in this reading that we catch a hint of the pain that Judas' betrayal caused, not only to Judas, but to Christ himself. And this was not just physical pain. It was the pain of heartbreak. Do we not here glimpse the infinite compassion that Christ must have had for Judas and, indeed, has for every human being? Such is what groaned in his bosom when, after Judas betrayed him with a kiss, he said, I believe with pathos unspeakable, "*Friend, why have you come?*"[1] Jesus pronounces woe upon Judas, not because he was made by a God who hated him, still less because he was predestined to suffer forever. Christ pronounces doom on Judas because of how low he had sunk, and how terrible his agony and self-loathing must one day be, when he came to see that he had freely betrayed one who loved him so dearly. What more terrible thing can befall a soul than to betray an innocent friend? Nay, not an innocent friend only, but a friend who loved so much that he would be willingly found guilty—would willingly be *crucified*—for his betrayer's sake. And yet before we pass judgment on Iscariot, let us look into our own hearts, friends, and see if we have not taken silver pieces from the world and helped drive nails through the hands of Jesus.

Note well my point. It is not to squabble about which interpretation of a verse in the Bible is correct. Indeed, for the purpose of my argument, I could be mistaken altogether, and Judas *could* have been divinely determined to betray Christ and so be consigned to an eternal hell because of it. At present, I mean only to show not the *right* meaning of a text, but the *possibility* of the *wrong* meaning of one. If it is so easy to misinterpret the very

---

1. Matt 26:50.

words of Christ and to draw from them implications so vastly different, we ought to approach the New Testament with a certain profound awareness of this fact.

Neither is my aim to cast doubt upon the inspiration of the Scriptures. Though, should such a doubt arise consequently from what I say, I would not for that reason be silent. There are far worse things than to doubt the infallibility of the Bible, friends. For assent as to inspiration is purely a matter of intellect, and may be held by even the most wicked-willed heart. The demons *believe* in God, you remember, yet that does not stay their hand; and many a man has tortured and enslaved and pillaged with the words of the New Testament on his lips. Yet I will go so far as to cast doubt upon, not the Bible, but our *understanding* of it, to say this. Unless you have asked yourself what you would do if were you to read something in it that contradicted your own purest notions of goodness and the loveliness of God and the greatness of the heart of Jesus Christ, and unless you have answered which you would trust—your own honest valuation of these things, or the words written down—you cannot advance in your knowledge of God or his truth.

Suppose you read in the New Testament something from the mouth of Christ that seemed to contradict your best and truest notions of what is best and true: yea, notions you may have heard from the mouth of Christ himself before. Suppose, for instance, that you were a modern Abraham who became convinced that God had commanded you to make a bloody sacrifice of your son, because of something you read in the Bible. Suppose also that you had been visited by an angel at your son's birth who told you to love him and raise him to be a good man, so he could love his God and your God. What would you do? What would you think? Here stand two contradictory revelations. You must choose one or the other.

Let us go further with the thought. Suppose you read in a letter of Paul some passage which seemed to logically imply that you ought to slay in your heart all love for your fellow human—humanity itself being a potsherd to be broken and cast aside at the arbitrary will of one to whom you must bow unquestionably in obedience. Would you slay humanity in your heart? Would you try to look upon it as if it were nothing more than valueless mud? It matters nothing to my purpose whether any texts in Scripture *actually* say such things. It only matters if they *could*. How far *can* the Bible go, fellow truth seeker, before it lies? What if it should contradict very truth itself? Which do you say ought to bow to the other: truth as it seems to thee, or as it reads on the page?

I ask again. What would you do if the Bible told you to murder every love and joy and dream you ever had, and to worship and adore all that seemed to you wicked? Would you turn to the commentary of some learned theologian, to see what mazes could be spun to make the text unsay what to you it so plainly does say? Would you go to some saint to get his spiritual understanding, to conform your mind to what he had of his own labor began to believe? And if so, what good would that do? Ah, you would take the whole question off yourself! You would have another answer it for you! You ought to know, friend, that the knowledge of God cannot be bought at that price, for it would rob it of its secret truth. The decision—the settling of the Question—must begin and end in you. *You* must think and feel and believe. If thou chooseth what seems to thee right and true, thou shalt be the better for it. If thou art mistaken, so long as thou followeth what thou seest to be his truth, his light, his will, the Lord of life and truth will set thee right. If this were not so, we could not trust him.

Again I say, the burden—the step out onto the shaky bridge of being—you must take up yourself, else the entire investigation, the entire reading of Scripture, the entire attempt to know God and be a disciple of Christ, the entire reason you have a soul and mind and will of your own, is no use. And besides, even supposing some deliverance did come on some difficult passage by some other person, are you to imagine that for every subsequent dilemma you will always be given similar clarity? A thousand dilemmas arise to the thinking mind that tries to understand the words of the New Testament and incorporate them into his being. The more one thinks honestly and the more one tries to be true—the more, that is, one seeks to take every thought of his brain captive to Christ and to have the spirit of the Son dissolve in his veins—the more the textual predicaments may appear. What shall he do? The questions sprout up infinitely.

There is no getting around the fact: at some point *we* must look at the puzzling thing ourselves. Things have not been settled by bygone thinkers. We must look out with our own eyes and speak our own judgment on the matter. It is time we cast our lot of faith with our *own* coin. What, would you have another live for you? Would you take out another's heart or brain and claim them as your own? Surely you know that they will not work for you, for they are not yours. Where would this stop? Would you have another raise your children for you or love your spouse for you? Would you have another direct the very impulses of your soul, yea, even the most religious and God-oriented? Would you, friend and seeker—if seeker you really be—would you have another be a child of God for you? Would you, who call yourself a Christian, have another look up into the face of Jesus for you? If you would give your spirit away to the thought and soul of another thinker, *who* in fact are you? Can you say that you even *are*?

It is dreadful thing, friends, to come upon the fact that we must *be*. For it means we must meet the burden of existence: we must wrestle it, cry out in our struggle against it, and grope for some solid ground on which to stand to fight it. I well remember the discovery—a metaphysical earthquake to the core of my being—that I was my own self, my own choosing me. There was the decision-crisis of *existence* laying in my lap, to do with what I would. Where should I turn with it? Who would take it from me? If no one, how should I direct my steps? Were not my choices infinite? Did everything not spread out like a limitless nothingness in front of me? I wanted so badly to give the whole thing to someone else! It was too terrible, too unknowable, too undetermined! And even supposing I could hand the reins to another, would it not still be me—myself—who did so? Alas, there was no escape! I thought: if there be a God, may he help me!

Yet for all that, the fact remained, staring unmovable. No other could take my place. It all comes back, unavoidably. We cannot escape our individuality, our own personal response to *being*—and thus to God. The sooner we admit this, the better, for the sooner we can cry out to that God as Father, knowing better our needy condition.

"Oh Lord, we live amid a nauseating uncertainty, reaching regions of profoundest obscurity in consciousness and feeling. How we wish for some sure footing on things, some pure light, some faith! Help us, Source of our souls, in such an existence, to stand with our chests out and our feet firmly planted. Help us have faith, and hope, and love! Help us, Lord, to be!"

Ah, brother! Ah, sister! Until you can see that you owe your allegiance first to what seems to you good and right and true and worthy, and only secondly to something else, and it only insofar as it gives you clearer light into what you can already see, you are a slave to the thoughts and religions of other minds. You are a slave to ideas which, for all you know, may not even have been in the head of those you think that they belonged to, or at any rate not with the implications that you extract from their words. I can well imagine meeting St Paul and describing to him the system that some theologian contrived out of the few letters of his that we have in our Bibles, with all that system's logical deductions. I can well imagine, I say, showing Paul such a thing, and hearing him exclaim "May it never be!" In Paul's own explication of his words, would he not, perhaps, reference other letters of his, myriads it may be, to modify and clarify those that have been twisted, much in the same way that we now use the Epistles of the New Testament to modify and clarify some passages of his, which, taken in isolation, appear absurd, or appear to contradict other truths found in Scripture? Did not Paul correct the Corinthians by telling them that they had read him wrong? Does he not say "when I wrote you last, I did *not* mean what you took me to mean! If I did, you would have to go out of the world to abide by my teaching!" [2]? It is Paul himself who shows us that it is possible to mistake him, to misunderstand him, to deduce some consequence he did not intend. Did Peter not say Paul wrote things "hard to understand" that some "twist to their own destruction"[3]? Then again I would not be surprised if the apostle could not quote a single line of his own inspired words in the sacred text, him having his essential life, every moment, by the Spirit rather than the letter. Perhaps the whole quest for a rigid systematizing of his writings would evoke from him the cry: "I decided to know nothing among you except save Jesus Christ, and him crucified!"[4]

Do not be afraid of this fact, but know it well, yet neither take it further than need be: the same book in thy hands called the Bible has done tremendous benefit to humanity; yet it has also done tremendous harm. In every age there are men and women who use it to justify actions which the best Christians in subsequent ages abhor with utmost loathing in the name of Christ. To whatever revelation or knowledge may exist in anyone, be he a Moses or a Paul, it does no good to the one who cannot understand what is said. In that sense—in *that* sense—it is useless, and serves only to darken the mind of the one who assents to what he does not see as true. Where truth is not seen but only sworn to in blind allegiance, there can exist nothing but falsity and dishonesty. Such serves but to increase doubt and build up plaque in spiritual veins that long to flow strong with the life-blood of Christ.

I have nothing to do with apparent discrepancies in the Bible regarding *facts,* such as whether Judas hanged himself, or fell from a cliff, or both. Rather, I speak here only of pictures of God which reflect his nature and the

---

2. 1 Cor 5:9-10
3. 2 Pet 3:16
4. 1 Cor 2:2

person of Christ. Let us go back to my initial hypothetical. Let us suppose Scripture says—which it does say—that God is light, and in him there is no darkness at all. Further, let us suppose that the Bible says—which it does say—that God is love, and desires all to be saved, and takes no delight in the death of the wicked, and that he is the universal Father who causes it to rain on the just and unjust alike. Here we have on one hand a scriptural *datum*—God's absolute loveliness and love for all. But let us suppose, on the other hand, that we read something in the Bible which seems to contradict this datum. Suppose, *hypothetically*, we were to read "God is darkness," or, "in him there is some darkness, for he is not pure light. He delights in the death of the wicked, and causes it to rain only on a few. " In other words, say we were to read in the Bible the perfect negation of what was before positively asserted.

I want only this hypothetical in the mind to bring out my point, which is this. If you cannot answer what you would do in the face of such a contradiction, you cannot really know the true God, if he exists. For where would you go to find goodness, if what you understood by that word became empty? You have not created your understanding of goodness. You simply find yourself with it inside, moving you, shining on you, refreshing you, directing you. How then can it blossom in you, if you deny the very root of its growth? Listen again to the Paul you have memorized. He says that by *rejecting conscience*, some have shipwrecked their faith. Faith therefore, and belief in God, depends on the reliability and testimony of conscience. Abandon it or suppose it a useless guide and, verily I say, on its voyage towards truth, your vessel will crash on the rocks.

A being to whom nothing is true or false, or everything true and nothing false, is a being unintelligible, for it may be true to deny of him in one breath what we affirm of him in the next. He could then exist and not exist, be all lovely and not all lovely, create and not create. If, therefore, God really is good and not evil, if he really is love and not hate, if he really is our Father and not the Devil, then certain things must be true of him and certain things false. He will *not* delight in suffering. He *does* desire all to be saved. But if we say that we cannot "really" know that God is what we mean by good, then, if God were in fact really what we meant by good, we would be paralyzed in principle from knowing so. We would negate the very thing necessary to gain knowledge in the first place: our own sense of goodness. Again, to learn what something is like is to be able to form some positive conception about that thing—to say things that are true and deny things that are false about it. But if, when we run into passages in the Bible that would seem, when taken to their conclusions, to make God's character no different than Satan's, and if we accept those passages as telling truths about God, even though they seem to us wicked, there becomes no possible way to differentiate God from Satan. We then can either form no positive conception of God, since anything at all may be true of him, or form no conception of him which is different from the most wicked being we can imagine. If we take this path, we have lost all ability to ever approach, let alone love and trust, a good God, if one exists.

Scripture cannot be higher than the God of Scripture. Therefore if our theory of the inspiration of Scripture leads us to conclude that God is not what we mean when we call him good and loving, may the real God help us find another theory of inspiration! For, if in fact God is good, then we have by a mere theory of inspiration forfeited the only real way we have of growing in our knowledge of him in the first place: looking with honest conscience for traces of that perfect Living Will which shines in our hearts.

Consider the following train of thought: a certain reading of Paul can imply that God has predetermined some of his creation to be eternally damned and suffer unimaginable torture, *apart* from and *before* any action on the part of the creature itself. On such a reading, the creature cannot help but go the fate that such a God predestined for it. Consequently, God *intends* this—to create beings in whom for all eternity he generates a necessary and infinite desire for himself, while also eternally decreeing never to give them the very thing he is creating them to want. Nor does this God take them out of existence. Rather he makes it something which itself deserves further punishment. Also, the torture of these souls serves to heighten the blessed in heaven who were arbitrarily spared a similar fate. Whatever ties of love those blessed in heaven had to the damned are turned into feelings of loathing, righteous hatred, and rejoicing in punishment. The child who sucked at the mother's breast, who now suffers the blackest, loneliest, most tormented and unfulfilled existence possible, becomes an object of perfect delight to that same mother, who sees the suffering of her child, and is *overjoyed*.

I ask, if *this* picture of God can be accepted while also maintaining that God is "love" and "good," *what possible picture of God could not be?* If you grant that God can torture sentient beings forever who he need not have created, yet whom he does create in order to suffer, and who, for that reason, cannot but be wicked, what possible moral action would be inconsistent with God's goodness? Could not such a being do anything at all and still be called loving and good? Such an approach to God, where one attaches any conceivable action to his character while automatically affirming that that character is "love" and "good," makes meaningless those very words. For they cannot carve out their own definition. They have nothing to resist them, therefore are meaningless. What then have we said—what have we meant—by calling God good and lovely?

Any idea of God or any theory about how we come to know him which destroys our ability to distinguish between good and evil and love and hate ultimately refutes itself. For if our theories of knowledge entail that we cannot know God's nature as positively good and infinitely trustworthy and altogether lovely, then, for all we know, God may punish us for doing exactly as he commands us in the very Bible which leads us to such questionable conclusions about him in the first place. Shall you trust the abductor who says "do this and your child shall live"? Given the nature of the criminal, is it reasonable—is it even possible—to *trust* him? How believe anything he says, except out of sheer terror and desperation? The final question is whether the belief in the *goodness of God* or that of the *infallibility of Scripture* is to prevail when they conflict. When the two are at odds, we must hold to the goodness of God. This is not to spite the Bible, but to honor the one who gave us the Bible. For accepting a notion of Scripture which entails that God may be evil or anything other than necessarily good denies the possibility of any such being as a good God who could give us the Bible for our benefit in the first place.

I know the weight and force of the Bible, brothers and sisters. I know the power and life it holds in many a mind and soul. I do not wish to dispute its inspiration with anyone. But I do wish to ask questions about possible implications of its words—at least as this or that person understands them. Does that trouble you, friend? Does it frighten you to suppose that the words on the page that you have held so dear and built up into a world-system of comfort and answers, may be such as to never have been uttered by the Lord, or thought by his followers? Does it bother you that the Bible is a thing that you *could be* mistaken about? Is the very hypothetical that I ask you to form, where you must ask yourself what you would believe were the Bible to say something false, is this very question something you shrink from, nay, cannot even possibly entertain? The true person will not shrink from true questions, though he may approach them with a soul trembling on the edge of the meaning-devouring abyss.

Do you, reader, sensing the truth approach— it may be in an uncomfortable question or unwanted logical deduction—do you shut the door of your mind and sit content with your old system? Do you seek comfort in your own small world, conceived and spun out of your own wishes, or the thoughts of other thinkers? Do you feel the claustrophobia of possible error, of the potential pain that truth herself may bring? Why do you fear? Know ye not that truth, being a blessed gift of God, wounds only to heal? Yea, even if we can but lie still while she works her fiery tongue in our bosom, she shall nonetheless work a mighty wonder. Oh weary soul, do you not long to cast off what *appears* true, so that you may hold of very truth *itself*? Surely you know that, you not facing the Question—that heart-fear of yours, whatever it is—does nothing to answer it. Doubt not that the Question must be answered someday by everyone, if everyone is to become true. Turning away from it now will not make it go away. Neither does it remove the fact that you are already doing the very thing you claim is too blasphemous to entertain. Or do you not think that you are already reading the Bible and taking some of it as it seems right to you, and leaving other things, as they seem too terrible? Do you pluck out your eye when you look with envy? And if you do not, is it not because, regardless of what the words say on the page, the Lord could not have meant *that?*

I repeat the Question: when the two conflict, what will you trust—the goodness of God, that is, Hope itself, or the Bible as it appears to you? The dilemma sits immovable, as uncompromising as the choice between life and death, between Christ and the world. One must wrestle-read the Word oneself, so as to answer the Question oneself. The conclusions of other people are immaterial if you cannot see, cannot *feel*, their conclusions yourself. Every book of theology could be piled on top of each other from the beginning of the world and such would not tip the scales one mite in favor of your *own* faith-answer. *You* must live and think and *be*.

My great cry to the Christian heart is this: what *could* the Bible say that you would not accept? Nothing at all? What if the Bible claimed that God was evil, that he hated his creation, yea, if it said that God did not exist? Would you still believe it then? If there is nothing that you would not accept and would not believe, I have no more words for you. He who can believe absolutely anything can believe absolutely nothing. He is not sturdy enough to stand up and walk of himself, let alone grapple and reason with. He is such as to hold that *either* his best *or* his worst notions are equally capable of describing the All-Perfect God. How could such a one be convinced—of anything?

Do I have to have a book to tell me to believe in an all-beautiful God? Verily, no. I say, if any book or any doctrine gave me a demon-god, a god who could create feeling beings who could not be happy unless he was by nature their Father, a god who shall torment souls for all eternity in the blackest nightmare a creatively omnipotent imagination could divine, that book or that doctrine would lie, and I would let it fall to the ground and leave it stuck in the dried mud of history. God is a God of the living. I feel him now in every smile, every warmth of heart, every joy and hope of human soul. Neither book nor doctrine can substitute the Spirit of the Living One, breathing life every moment into my being!

Perhaps, reader, you are such as to say that you have never yet come across a passage in the Bible which seemed inconsistent with what your God-given conscience tells you is good and true and lovingly beautiful. If that be honestly so, I have no more to say to you. If you have not found any such thing, you may yet, if you come to the Word seeking answers to the questions of life. All I say is, when or if you meet the Question, I call upon you to answer it honestly and truthfully. And if you never come to such a crisis, blessed art thou! For you shall never be in danger of listening falsely, since the dilemma on which the whole problem arises will never be before you.

All who follow Christ must ask themselves: am I being a true soul—a true lover and seeker after truth? Do I desire it with my whole being? To all who answer yes, we are brothers and sisters and, truly, we fight on the same side, however we may disagree. May the Son of Man come quickly, find the faith in our hearts strong and pure, and so lead us home. Full of such trust may we "the sheep follow him, for we know his voice" (John 10:4–5).

3

A Stranger They Will Not

"When he has brought out all his own, he goes before them, and the sheep follow him, for they know his voice. A stranger they will not follow, but they will flee from him, for they do not know the voice of strangers."

JOHN 10:4–5

THE IMAGE OF CHRIST as a shepherd and we his sheep is unique as an image of tenderness and love, specifically because it points to our ignorance of, and at the same time, innate trust in Christ. There is also the fact, sweet beyond utterance, that the shepherd's desire to lead his sheep is so strong that he is willing to lay down his life for them. In leading his sheep, the shepherd shall give up all that he has. They are not therefore something he is indifferent to, mere objects which would not bother him if they were to go astray. They are worth the very life of Jesus himself.

I believe that there was never a lover of human person more tender than Jesus, for all human tenderness meets an infinite wellspring of love in him. All self-sacrifice, all gladness in beholding the happiness of the beloved, all swelling and burning of the breast towards the other, all aches for unity and friendship and closeness and comfort, yea, all willingness to go to the extremity of action and conscious feeling: all these things have an endless existence in the heart of Christ.

Ears of Corn

In the image of us as sheep we see a profoundly simple reason why we follow the Lord. We follow him because we know his voice. But what does it mean, friends, to know the voice of the Lord? Ah, we *do* know what it means. And yet, who can give proper utterance to the thing? To know the voice of the Lord is to hear him and *feel* that *it is he*. I say, to know the voice of Christ is to hear in the depths of one's being a voice which, for the moment (it may be the most fleeting of moments), rises above others and asserts itself by the conviction of its own essential life. The mode in which we hear this voice is, and must be, infinitely variable: now in the dim recesses of conscience; now in the face of a loved one; now in the words of the New Testament; now in some expression of nature. Through all these channels of the spirit flow the same life-water that comes from the one rock of Christ.

It is no surprise that the sheep in this passage, since they are sheep, have no conscious awareness of the voice that they know. They do not hear the voice of the Lord and reflectively think, "Now, this could either be the voice of the shepherd, or the voice of a stranger. However, based on theory x and y, and y and z, therefore, we conclude, it is probably the shepherd. Therefore we will go ahead and follow him." No. Sheep do not think that way. They simply hear the voice and, knowing it, follow it. How many will come at length to realize that, though they thought they were following the voice of Jesus, they were in fact following only their own voice which they dressed up and justified to themselves as the voice of Jesus! How many have supposed that their own voice sounded enough like the voice of Jesus that it made no difference to them whether they should make an honest inquiry of the fact! Why then, since they are indifferent to the truth, should they be troubled about discovering it? How little some care to hear the voice of Christ!

I do not say we should never test the spirits. We must weigh very carefully all the things that we believe about our Lord and his God. I mean only to remind us that there is a path to life in this single aspect of faith which, in principle, cannot be walked any other way. I am speaking of hearing the Lord and feeling, prior to any reflection, that it is the Lord, and then assenting to him and following him and *being* in him, before all second thoughts and what-ifs and self-deluded justifications spring up into the mind.

The Lord came to make us into such as we would have a will fully one with his, and therefore with his Father's also. Jesus came to make us one with God—*his* God—the one whom Paul said we cry to as "Abba!"[1] Is not

---

1. Gal 4:6

the great Spirit of our Infinite God being ever-poured into our hearts, so that one day we may be fully consciously one with him? God's will is always for us; yet our will is not always for us. For that to be we must make our will one with his. But to be so united with God requires us to hear and follow and *be*. When we hear him speak to us—when we feel him tugging at our hearts and feel that it is he—our first impulse should be to *let him have his way*.

I well know all the criticisms that attend such a view. It is indeed very dangerous—dangerous for the individual and dangerous for humanity. Dangerous for the individual: for who knows what the Lord will ask of him? Dangerous for humanity: for, since the race is not all of one mind, discord will necessarily arise. Brother may think the worst of brother, and one's best friend may become his bitterest foe. That is as it must be, until all the flock comes in. Besides, is not the danger in the opposite direction greater? For which would you be: one who follows his own conscience—prays and thinks and *does* as honestly as he might with the light that he sees—one who trustfully lets God set right all else that is wrong; or one who, never making up his mind whether what he sees is light or a mere sunspot in his own eye, never goes about trustfully responding to anything he feels upon his heart? Or what of one who, not seeing a light at all, tries to convince himself, perhaps from the testimony of others, that he does see light? Is not the honest thinker who confesses darkness better than he? What would it matter, even if the other who he blindly followed was a saint—even the Son of Man—if with his own eyes the man did not see the truth himself? Surely nothing, else it would be better to lie to oneself than to be true to oneself. The one who moves when God nudges—or moves even when he *thinks*, it may be mistakenly, that God is nudging—is the one most likely to grow in the right direction. However many missteps he makes along the way, he has still, at least, set off walking the path of faith on his own feet.

This is how Christ goes before us as our shepherd, giving us a way to live. He tells us this one great truth: God is thy Father: listen to him. And we his sheep, with slow yet trusting hearts, hear this and *know* it, and try to follow his lead. Could Jesus have given humanity a better message than this: that we all have a loving Father, and that our one way to life was to do all that lay on our heart to be at one with this Father, and to love our neighbors as ourselves?

Although the *following* we do is of the utmost importance—indeed, it is the very sap and lifeblood of our being—our Lord here speaks another truth, equally necessary. He tells us that his sheep do not follow a stranger. Rather, they flee. And why? Because they do not know the stranger's voice. Yet there are metaphysicians, some with the best of intentions, who tell us, in so many words, that God is the *strangest* of all beings. At most we can but negate God—to say what he is not. For any notion that we have, we must ultimately say, "God is not that." To such thinkers I ask: did Jesus Christ ever suggest—ever even come close to suggesting—that his Father was like *that*? What would it mean, if he called God Father, but God was not really our Father? Is God himself less than essential Fatherhood? Surely if he was, surely if God was a purely negated abstraction, Christ would have told us? And if Christ did not, was he not then mistaken in his own conception of the Supreme Being, therefore no true teacher of how humanity can be at one with the Divine?

No doubt we cannot comprehend God, and no doubt our concepts and words point to some reality far too grand to grasp in single utterance or finite human thought. But we do have some true notion of God. Surely, if we claim to follow Jesus, we can say more than simply what God is not! A God that we can describe in no other way than abstract negations is a God that has not been described. In what way have we distinguished him from nothing, from non-entity? We end with a concept either meaningless or unknowable. Yet who can love the meaningless or unknowable? Does not desire presuppose, if not certain knowledge, at least something apprehended as desirable? For desire to exist, the loved thing must be some way *in* the desiring one. To be wanted at all, a thing must *somehow* be felt and sensed and known. If this is not true, what remains for love to hold onto and spend itself on? The mind hands to the heart a mere nothing, and the heart simply stares, and then cries out for its God.

The soul cannot love that which does not at least seem lovely to it. The mind cannot contemplate what is to it an absolute unknown and unknowable. For after negating all positives and abstracting away all meaning, what is left to think about—to love? For love to love, it needs Love Essential. But where is this? Where is the soul's God? *Dear God*, it cries, *are you there? Can I know you, can I love you at all?* In reaction to its inability to know and therefore love, the soul vomits forth upon the unknown its own self-reflected consciousness, feeling never closer to the truth. If God is not Primordial and Necessary Love, as understood, however dimly, by the soul, then there is nothing in human consciousness that reflects a primordial and necessary loveliness. Since it cannot touch its God, all that the soul knows is God's negation: "that which is not God, not Love Essential." That which flickers across its brain which it calls love is no grander than any other emotion produced by some movement of atoms. The soul asks, "Is what I call my God simply a mirrored reflection of my own claustrophobic self out onto a blank heartlessness?" How terrible the thought! Who hopes in God but does not also hope that God is the ultimate deliverance of the self from the self, not the banishment of the self to itself forever!

I have the greatest reverence for all those ancient thinkers who say that God is "beyond being," and who proclaim that all we can know of God is what he is not. But at the same time my heart cries to them: what good to me is a God I cannot know, a God whose essence lies inaccessible behind what is and must forever be either a false appearance, or the negation of all that ever could appear to me? I need more than a being indistinguishable from the void, a being that I cannot even in principle know! Surely we must have some feeling of God himself, not merely as we perceive him, but as he is! Surely we must be able to form some true notion of him, however vague and misty! We cannot be left with the worship of nothing, or of our own selves writ large! Oh friends, do we not need a Father? A Father we may never fully comprehend, but a Father still that we may know, that we may touch, that we may find our home in?

What in God we do not know, we fail to know out of a familiarity and closeness that we cannot articulate, not a chasm of infinite darkness which appears no different than the abyss of non-entity. Verily, the real God must be grander than what we know of his Fatherhood—but for all that, nothing less than the perfect Father. Whatever else, a stranger will not do. However such may sound to you, dear brother or sister, I know no other voice.

"Ah," one says, "by desiring such a human notion of God, you are saying nothing about God himself. You are only proving your own need to be needed."

What other human description of God can there be but that which necessarily supposes humanity's absolute *need* of God? If there is a God at all, is not a human being that which necessarily depends on him utterly, every moment of its existence? Of course my description of the Divine proves my need to be needed! God forbid it should not! I ask, is your God—that god in whom you ask me to believe—anything less than the All-Relating which my soul needs? If so, I say, away with the falsity! Must not our God be big enough to fulfill my longing? Does not my longing exist for no other reason than to be fulfilled by him? But then God *must* be the All-Beautiful

God, the Everything of my hopes and imaginings. Indeed and infinitely more! Be gone with the god who *may* be, who *could* be all lovely! The only God great enough to be our God is one who could not fail to be himself, could not fail to be infinitely lovely and loving!

The more the soul needs its God, the more it must be dissatisfied with anything less than the All-Relating and All-Perfect. An existence which does not offer the greatest God imaginable is an unbearable, hopeless existence, forever less than what the soul infinitely needs. Take away the All-Relating, or give me a doctrine which implies anything less, and you murder the only God that can be a God to my longing soul. Would you take away my bread and hand me a stone? Would you destroy the only possible home for my pilgrim spirit and tell me I can dream up a God greater than the real God, thereby showing that the god you give me in his place is no God at all?

I ask, what heart can say it is content to be the child of a God that does not care for it; nay, a God that is indifferent to whether it exists? How can a human heart love, how can it find its fulfillment in, a heartless God—a God who has no heart of love himself for his creature's heart? Here is a God that has made creatures for some purpose they cannot tell, or perhaps for no purpose at all, which amounts to the same! How then is he a real God to what he made? How can that heart-need which longs to be loved by its God ever be met, if God does not love that heart from himself: that is, from *his* heart? The one grand dream of the soul is to be *known* by *its God*. Shall God never know it? Who does not yearn beyond all depths of feeling to hear his Maker say, "Well done, *my child*"? Such single phrase, such single thought in the heart of the Father of Jesus Christ, would be enough to justify all the woes of life. It is a declaration nothing less than the soul's eternal life and joy and bliss forever. For in it, the soul knows that its being is essentially related to and rooted in the Divine Love itself. In this declaration it knows that God is its Father, and it is his child.

I ask, who made this desire for a Father in us? If we need to be needed, wherefore? We did not cause our own neediness. We come into the world needy already, without our choosing. Who would dispute that we exist as one great, infinite need: one vast yearning for *more*? Such is the way it must be. Yet this state—this *must be*—must also have come from God, from the hand of the Maker. How else could it be?

I ask, would a good God make such a need and such needy beings, unless he planned on meeting it and fulfilling them? An unknowable god may—for that matter, an unknowable god may do anything, and as such is not worth worshiping, for he may damn you for doing the very things which he commands you to do, his character being as equally unknowable as his nature. But what about an all-perfect Father? Would he create a need that went unfulfilled? What could human heart ever hope for or desire, that the one God had not made it hope for and desire in the first place? But then would an all-perfect God not have also made the *fulfillment* of the hopes and desires that he first implanted in his children? Are we to suppose God creates a hungry belly but no food to fill it; that he creates a yearning of the spirit of which there is no nectar of satisfaction? *Never*. If he has made the belly, he has made the food as well! If he has made the desire, so also has he made the fulfillment! Ah, friend! Can you see it? The greater our desires, the greater the goodness of God. The greater the goodness of God, the greater our confidence that our very desires themselves have been created for no other reason than to be filled by God. The whole purpose for our state of yearning and wanting is simply so that one day we can possess what we most yearn for and need! What a hope: to be loved into being by an all-loving God!

Surely no one will tell me that I *ought* to believe in a God I cannot know? Does my eternal salvation or earthly happiness depend on believing in an unknowable, a thing of which I can form no notion? What kind of obligations do I have—*could* I have—towards such a thing? How can I trust in an incomprehensibility in order to give it my obedience, not to say *trust*? Can I love a nothingness to give it my heart faithfully?

Some theologians say that the creation makes no difference to God, that the whole thing could be consigned to an eternal hell or raised to an infinite heaven and in either case you have the same God. God would still be God, whether all his children were lost, or all were perfected in loving glory. Do these thinkers not contradict Jesus Christ, who says that it pleases the Father to give the flock a kingdom? Do they not depart from the apostle Paul, who says that God long-suffers with his creatures? How can a Father be indifferent to his flock? How can a God who suffers long with his creation, be careless if they perish? See the danger in taking one's eyes off the Father and Son, and letting them linger on some other thinker or system—rooted, it may be, in the profoundest knowledge of metaphysics, yet not consciously nourished by the divine-human relation!

The god of the pagan Greeks is often reduced to an unrelated abstraction. It is too little mentioned that Aristotle held that God neither knew the world nor loved it. This is because he knew well enough the logic of his metaphysic—far better, I think it obvious to say, than many Christian successors who attempted to Christianize his philosophy. For if God—the *actus purus*—knew the world, this would entail an essential relation in the divinity to the creation. That is, God's knowing the world would entail that he essentially and necessarily loved the world, and that this love and knowledge would be in him his own perfection. But this would mean that God's existence was constituted and therefore perfected by, his creating, knowing, and loving the creature. In a word, if the god of Aristotle knew the world, it would entail, not his essential unrelation, but his essential all-relation: that is, his essential Fatherhood.

Therefore for the Greek thinker, since God was unrelated to the world, he could neither know it nor love it. Aristotle may be forgiven for his conception of the deity, although that may be a hard forgiveness, since verily he had Plato to teach him. But what of us Christians, who have the Word made flesh, and call Jesus Christ our elder brother? What of us who, at least, though we may not say we fully *believe* in a God of love, at least *hope* that one exists? Where is our excuse? If I was not a Christian, or if Christianity was to me impossible to believe, I may well hold to such a view: an all good *actus purus*, never knowing nor loving the world, yet ever drawing it towards itself, with the world, always straining for union and perfection, being never able to attain it. The transcendence of the *all-good* of the eternally perfect would overcome the nihilism of the *never-being-able-to-attain* of the eternally imperfect. To believe that *something* existed absolutely full, itself subsistent life and being and joy, would be better to believe than that the good as such was not strong enough *to be* eternal.

But how much better to believe the Christian idea that we are all children of God! How much better to believe that we are all, as the psalmist says, God-like offspring of the Most High![2] Thank God we have the words of the Bible in front of us, and that which is self-evident within us, which proclaim that humans were *made* in the *image of God*. Thank God we have the Spirit of our Maker, our highest God, that being of subsistent life, who testifies with our spirit, and groans within us with words unspeakable! Thank God we have the utterance of the apostle Paul, who said that what awaits us is a glory unspeakable: one that has not even entered into human heart to conceive. Thank God we have Jesus Christ, who delivers us from profoundest nihilism yawning wide when we contemplate the possibility of an indifferent and unrelated deity, and who puts in its place an essential Fatherly divinity!

2. Ps 82

To believe that the world makes no difference to God is to say that all that is not God—and, therefore, all that *is* the world—is valueless. To say God is unrelated to the world is to set God's face eternally against creation. It is to say, in a word, that God neither knows nor loves the world as a thing worthy of attention. Indeed it is to equate humanity with absolute nothingness. If God is indifferent to creation, then it becomes less than that which arouses anger in a righteous, or even wicked heart. Creation becomes something worse than something hateful: it becomes nothing. The eyes of the alien—the *unfatherly*—deity take no notice of it: indeed *can* take no notice of it, for that would require that he was essentially related to it.

But only a God who did not have a heart could have such an unfatherly unrelation to creation. If our God has a heart for his creation at all, must he not be *essentially*, in the very perfection of his being, *our* Father?

Note well the problem. It is not that those things the uncaring and heartless deity makes *may* be eternally lost in hell fire or annihilation. It is that they ever *could* be. It is that the God who gives them being is such that it *could* make no difference to him, one way or the other, to call a created soul into existence, infuse it with hope of heaven and love of neighbor and desire for deepest joy, and then annihilate or torment it indifferently. This god would be just as satisfied with, and find just as tolerable, either way of things. If *this* is the god who rules the universe, the relation between it and us is already incapable of being sure and true, therefore impossible to mend, impossible to build on in faith and trust. How do you *love* that which is necessarily indifferent to your existence, your happiness, your love?

What would it matter whether *in fact* this god's creatures go wrong, if he does not care if they *shall*? Once God's infinite concern for us is gone, so too is our God, the only God who can truly save us—the God we infinitely need! If his universe is such—or if *he* is such—that we really could be indifferent to him, how could we ever rise to the level of significance ourselves? In his eyes our happiness does not rise to the level of notice, for we are, in the most metaphysically literal sense of the word, worthless, valueless, yea, being-less to him. If we are absolutely worthless to God, how could we be worth anything to each other? How can the valuation of the creature rise above that which the Creator has given to it? If *God* deems us worthless, worthless we must be!

What a lonely, meaningless, hopeless life: to be constantly killing and careless of the things we come to love! Everything we meet, all that delights us and gives us joy, whatever we find necessarily lovely, would be, in the eyes of God, something that may as well have never been! Why then ought the things we love endure? Why then should we care that they do? Why pray for thy friend, let alone thy enemy, if God does not care for either? If God could damn or save each indifferently, then each one is an indifferent thing. Why let thy heart groan for thy wife's salvation, or thy child's, or thine own? Why pray for any goods to accrue to thy fellow creatures? Would not such be an offense against the objective un-worth of their lives, their existence? Would not the desire of a loved one's salvation be a sin, an inappropriate valuation given to created being which ought not to be given to it, akin to wishing that the wicked man be rewarded for his wickedness or the good man punished for his righteousness? How deem necessarily valuable that which is necessarily worthless? Where would the appropriate valuation come from, if not from God, who himself is indifferent to the creature? At the very least our feeling of humanity's value must be an error, a misinterpretation of reality! If the whole human race could as easily perish in oblivion or be sentenced to eternal pain, then not one of us, in either our most pitiable condition or most noble, is worth the dignity of a sigh, let alone a tear! For God, who gives all creatures their objective value, has not invested any with an objective value that *he* recognizes!

Do you say that, in fact, God has so invested, at least *some* of his creatures, the dignity of being his children? I say, if we do not come into the world already naturally children of God, this does not remove the difficulty. For until such an *act* on God's part, no human being is worthy of love. Yet then, for every child born, if we consider them not yet children of the Father, we ought not desire their continuance—not to say salvation—since in themselves they are not *naturally* worth loving, worth perfecting, worth the glory of heaven! God must *additionally* bestow that worth on it, *after* the creature already exists! And this, some say, God may not do! He could look at the same creature, now already here, now already existing in the world, and say "I shall let it return to the dust. It is not worth giving eternal life." Thus—goodbye human race! In my heart I believed you an eternally good thing, a good thing from the mere fact that you *were*, that you came from God. But, from the moment you were thrown unwillingly into the mystery of existence, you were no higher than the nothingness out of which you came.

Oh God, may such a thing not be! If so, goodbye new formed eyes of the child, opening for the first time! Goodbye family with bonds as hard as iron, and roots as deep as oak tree! Goodbye joyful laugh of friend, and tender gaze of lover! Farewell ties of youth and old acquaintance, barely remembered, but longed to be renewed! Since none of you are worth anything in yourselves, why ought I defy the almighty pronouncement of your insignificance? Indeed is it not my duty to bend my conscience to his will, which is law? I must therefore become such that I do not care for you! It must be nothing to me that the things I have loved I have wanted to be saved, since nothing I have loved is inherently worth salvation! What then were the feelings I had towards you, my loves? Mistakes and misreadings? Delusions self-imposed and pathetically desired?

Such a metaphysic, where God can pass any human by as something unworthy of his continued, yea, eternal attention, is compatible with any revelation of God concerning his creation, is it not? What a woefully useless theology: one that leads equally to universal hope or universal despair; a theology that can hope everything of God, or nothing of him! The very same God could owe everything to his creature—that is, could owe his very self to it—or nothing, or only eternal pain!

Not saintliest monk in barest cell has ever fully sacrificed God's creation in honor of what he deemed the absolute will of such an unknown deity. Let him who has had a glimpse of such a soul-crushing cosmos put before him as a horrid possibility confess, that to think that God is nothing but an Unknowable is to think that God may be the most terrible demon imaginable. Such a God may demand anything. It may demand, not the outward murder of thy brother or sister, but what is far worse: their inward murder. It may demand that the heart no longer care whether brother or sister or father or mother find bliss in heaven or torment in hell. Such a God may demand that all the soul's relations be utterly negated and deconstructed, that they become merely *indifferent* to it. On and on, it may command, one after the other, the slaying of every precious thought that has ever swept across the beating heart, until precious things no more exist. And what can it do then? To what Father will the soul cry, since its universe is ruled by an Infinite Uncaring?

To suppose such a god is even *possible* is to suppose that one's highest duty in life *may be* to kill all one's hopes and cares and joys and loves, and to be content with an eternity of nothingness, with all one's friends and loves having returned to the abyss—if, indeed, they ever existed! Maybe they were dreams, mere atoms in a void, sent by the mocking demon-god? Where would the limit of infinite pain and torment be drawn, which such a god could not without question impose? Even the faintest hope, however small a joy, may be nothing but one more illusion of meaninglessness to murder on the altar of obedience to the Unknowable.. Words cannot put into feeling such a nihilism—such an absolute negation of meaning—that results from a theology that denies our God's essential and necessary Fatherhood. The unknown god, precisely because he is unknown, and, what is more, because in principle he *cannot* be known, is for that reason capable of whatever supposed harm or wickedness the mind can imagine. For there is nothing *certainly* known about him that prevents *anything* from being true of him. There is no *necessary* good to prevent some *possible* bad. To say there is some standard to which the unknown god approximates and which somehow limits his commands is to already suppose that such a god is not really unknown, but known, at least this much. Ask, could God create a world in which he commands all souls to do what is impossible for them to do, and still damn them for not doing it? If he cannot, then there you have it. He is at least known in this respect: he cannot do something *that* terrible. At least *that* is incompatible with his nature. But if God can do anything conceivable—and an Unknown-Almighty *can* do anything conceivable, that being the definition of the phrase—then no such limit exists. No essential Fatherhood can be invoked as a backstop.

The whole problem is in the *may be*. If God *may be* something else than necessarily an all-good parent to his creatures, then it is *possible* that such a horrible demon-god exist. But how can it even be possible that God not be God? Must the real God not really *be* God, that is, the God of his creation?

To suppose an unknown god exists, is the same as to suppose that any being you can imagine may exist: therefore no being, or the most terrible. Once the possibility is introduced, once the necessarily All-Perfect is lost, it makes no difference. But then the worst imaginable world may indeed be this world. For why wouldn't it be, seeing as the being who made it had no reason to make a world in which anyone is ever eternally happy anyway? How can one trust a being like that, a being who may indifferently damn him, a being who may have created him simply to love things in life, and then commanded him to deny his love for them, until he can no longer love anything at all? It would be as rational to trust in a fiction of one's own wishful thinking, and worship the fiction.

I say that to believe in any God less than a God of infinite relation and concern is worse than to believe in no God. For to believe in an unrelated god is to believe in the antithesis of God. It is to believe in a god of death, a god of annihilation, a god of nothingness. It is to believe that the necessarily All-Perfect is possibly imperfect; the essential *most* a potential *least*. Thank Jesus Christ that the God of the Bible pours out created goods on humanity, knowing that humanity is perfected by its very act of loving these things themselves. Our God says himself that it is not *good* for man to be alone. *He is pleased with us; he finds us valuable. He* says that the creation was made *very* good. From the foundation of the world, with the great Father-heart that he has necessarily, our God says: "I shall see the travail of my soul and be satisfied."

All things necessarily spring from God, from the abundant hand and care of the Father. Therefore, each thing made must have, somehow, God himself in it. In the same way that a newborn soul has a piece of its parent, so too must a piece of God be in everything he has made. I do not mean a physical, material piece: for what parent thinks that the spirit of his child has a piece of his own spirit physically? I mean something like a piece of his personality. Each creature of God has a bit of his infinite personality. Thus God in knowing creation must see his own beauty and goodness in each created thing, each uniquely mirrored God-speck of wondrous life-being. For the creation is God's gift of himself, to himself; and in his pouring out of himself onto himself, he thus gives himself to himself in infinite variety. For this reason God must love each created thing; for in loving each thing, he is loving himself. For God not to care about what he has made, or for him to be indifferent to it, would be for him to be careless or indifferent towards himself, towards his divine self-reflection. Such would be for the image he made not to bear the image of himself, which cannot be.

If we did not at least somewhat reflect God, we could not exist at all. That which is the utter opposite of God is not a creature, but non-entity. The negation of absolute being is not finite being, but non-being. Created being is no doubt different than uncreated being, but both still have *being* true of them. So long, then, as we are beings, we at least in that degree exist as an *icon* of God, and therefore as something that he loves.

Brothers and sisters, do not believe low things about our God. Believe in no God a thousand times faster than let your mind suspect that there exists a God that is indifferent to the world. Does the notion creep into thy thought, perhaps against thy will? So be it. Do not give it dignity enough even to alarm you. The thing is absurd. And even if it were not, what would be the point in believing it? If God does not care about you, what would it avail you to believe in some notion of him arrived at by argument? Do you think your *assenting* to the existence of such a god would make him care about you *more*? As if from the fact of your *believing* you were worthless you would *become* worth something!

Ears of Corn

If we cannot believe that God loves us with an infinite, unfailing fatherly love, what hope is there for us? Who are we to trust in, and where are we to turn? Certainly not to some abstract concept, taken out of proportion and to extremity, that defines God such that he can no longer be thought of as a *who* but simply as an *it*. Nay, if we are to *trust* in a God at all, it can only be in the God of Jesus Christ—*the* Father, the All-Related, the Infinitely-Concerned. But if then we trust in this God, God must be himself worthy of our trust: yea, infinitely so. It is only God's necessary Fatherhood, and the impossibility of him being anything else *to* anything else, that gives us any ground for our hope. For if God can even possibly be otherwise, our hope can possibly be groundless.

Surely no one will say that Christians must believe, on pain of damnation, that there is no reason to hope that such a being exists as we understand by the notion of a *necessarily All-Perfect Father*? And yet, that is all we need, friends. The smallest crack, however faintly we perceive the light shining through, will allow us to trust that what we see with squinting eyes of hope, may be more glorious than we can imagine. Let unwavering certainty and metaphysical systematizing wait—until the next world, if need be. Let us find whatever space we need to make hope possible, and our spirits shall not fail us.

If you desire this not, brother or sister, so be it. I have no more to say to you, nor care to incite further argument. What I write is not for your kind, at least not yet. I speak to those who yearn to be closer to the Spirit of that one who was and is "the reflection of God's glory and the exact imprint of God's very being."

4

The Reflection

"He is the reflection of God's glory
and the exact imprint of God's very being."

HEBREWS 1:3

LOOK YOUR SOUL LOOK nakedly in the face and ask it: why do you believe that the Word became flesh? Answer yourself honestly—for who else shall you deceive? Why do you call yourself a Christian?

All answers, save one, are destructible. All answers, save one, are but stunted reaches towards our highest calling and our greatest bliss. The one unshakable, the one undefeatable, is this. We believe that the Word became flesh because we believe that Christ reveals the one great truth of existence: that the human condition is a revelation of God. Christ shows us that to be living in the essential humanity of himself is to partake of the divine nature. To believe this is to call yourself a Christian.

Do you think you could be a Christian because an authority showed you a chain of arguments that demonstrated beyond doubt that some man two thousand years ago came back to life after he was crucified? Or do you suppose you could be a Christian because your father or mother was one, or a tradition of thinkers, or those you admire who have gone before you? Do you think, reader, that you could be a Christian because you are afraid to be anything else? As if your fear of unexplored regions of thought has any bearing on their truth or falsity! No, friend. You cannot be a Christian, that is, a *true* Christian, for such reasons. For that matter you cannot be a true *anything* for such reasons, for they are not true enough to make you true.

To be a Christian and to have the spirit of Jesus Christ in you is to feel and trust that every human being is a glory of God; that each person is of infinite and immeasurable value—yea, that even in yourself there dwells the inexhaustible riches of eternal love and life and divinity. Unless you believe that God is goodness and loveliness and life, and that the essential humanity of Jesus Christ is one with this and is working in you—unless you believe that the human condition is an ever-growing, ever-expanding participation in the divine—you build your house upon the sand.

To the thinker who would dispute me and claim between the divine and human an infinite, unrelatable gulf, I ask: what is God? Life, you say, or Goodness, or Love, or Happiness. You may say God is Intellect and Will and Freedom. You may go even to the most all-encompassing description: God is *Being* itself. Give whatever definition you please. I ask: are we not living? Are we not good? Have we not loved or been happy? Have we not intellect and will and freedom? Indeed, are we not *beings*? You see therefore that any word we give to God, we give because we have already partaken of the reality that the word signifies. Otherwise, we could not give the word. Our words would be meaningless when applied to God if the conscious experience we have, which we delimit and reproduce with them, was wholly inapplicable to God.. Either we would be denying what we mean by the term when applied to Him, or we would affirm the meaning and deny that that is what we meant when said of God.

Thus we are, in the recesses of our being, far deeper than argument or even word can touch, *necessarily* acquainted with God. We know and feel him even before we name him, for we necessarily participate in him simply by existing. Is not to be at all to be rooted in God and drawing one's life and reality altogether from him? We are, in absolute totality, whether consciously or unconsciously, whether in strength or weakness, bliss or pain, belief or despair, altogether in the living God. He is always and everywhere welling up inside us and spilling out of us and filling every nook in our soul.

To understand this is to understand that humanity is an image, a relation, a *reflection* of God. How then could there be an infinite gulf between us and him? To what greater universe would we put the *relata* of God and man, in which we stated that, though the two entities existed, they were

The Reflection

wholly unlike one another? And how would such a picture not itself be a diminution of God, a *placing* of him alongside the creature? How, if the two faces of divinity and humanity are eternally unrelated, would they not both exist within another, bigger God? It is absurd to think that some reality could exist unrooted in God, himself the Infinite and Unconditioned which contains all finites and conditions. Where would such a thing come from, except the Eternal?

If we must be able to penetrate the mysteries of creation and the self-existence of God in order to have faith and hope and peace and joy, we are of all creatures most pitied. Yet—although we cannot plumb the depths to the bottom, we can squint our eyes just enough to let a hint of the infinite light shine through, and warm our hearts.

Here is the great truth of the Incarnation: humanity gives us the face of God. That is, human nature shows us the divine nature in its own humanly unique way. All natures, I believe, reveal God. God is, I think, incarnate in every nature. For what is a nature but a thought-work of the divine? But if a thought-work, then also a reflection. No nature shows us God as he is in himself, for God in himself cannot be contained by the mind of creature, nor shown in full in singular revelation. Expression, as description, as apprehension, always delineates, always makes finite. But God—that Infinite in which all finite reality is—cannot so be expressed *as God*, that is, as Infinite Being itself. Therefore each of the expressions of God becomes to us a description of him. And our descriptions are just us taking a single image and mapping it on an infinite reality which cannot be exhaustively defined by a single image. We are like one lying cold in bed who, when he pulls the blanket to cover his neck, straightway exposes his feet.

Verily thou art a God who hideth himself, dwelling in light unapproachable, ever in the mind's periphery! Every attempt of thy creature to define thee is an attempt to lay hold of that which it cannot fully grasp! Yet still it believes that thou art the Great Warm Secret in everything!

Human feelings are things—they are person-experiences, come somehow from God's heart. Therefore God, being all good, must infinitely and perfectly account for them. In a word, he must *make good* of them. Since they are all rooted in his perfect goodness, so too must he be a perfect God to them. In Christ, God has revealed himself in the human experiences of suffering, pain, crucifixion, and death, and shown that these give way to a rising and a triumph. If God accounts for all pain, friend, he also accounts for the overcoming, conquering, and reconciling of all pain. If pain and suffering exist in Christ, and Christ is humanity united to divinity, then these very experiences that make up the life of Jesus and which saturate the human condition, must somehow be brought into an unimaginable flower of life. In Jesus, no bad experience, no horrible feeling, no loss of good, can ever be final. All are oriented towards the higher end which they serve.

If you do not believe this, why do you believe in the Incarnation at all? How could Christ be worth believing in unless he was himself the *triumph over pain*? Should we believe that the human God—and all humans that are related to him, which is to say, the whole human race—could be finally destroyed by suffering? That would be to assert that death is stronger than life: yea, that evil is stronger than good! Even if it were so, what good would it be to believe this? Suppose for the nihilist's sake that, at the very root of being, there exists eternal death and the negation of value. Why submit to it? Because it is true? But that has not been proven. Nor would it matter if it was, as loyalty to truth is simply one more assertion of the primacy of the good—of life and being—over against negation and death.

Or should we think that God is indifferent to pain, it being something somehow not sprung from him? Yet how then could it exist; how could it be? No, brothers and sisters. We must either believe that the source of our life and all that surrounds us and the destination towards which we move is all-perfect, gloriously beautiful, and lovely; or we must be like the Nordic men of old who fought against the gods, knowing that the destruction of their world could not be overturned. If we shall not go down fighting, if we shall not go down believing in the good and the true, why should we *be* at all? To be is to be *for something*. Therefore we cannot be—we cannot believe in—nothing. Thus, God, who is the ultimate justification of our being, must be, and must be all that he can be, all that we can conceive him to be. He must be infinitely perfect, beautiful, good, lovely, true. Else he is not strong enough to justify our own hopes, our own faith, our own act of *to-be-for-something*. The impulses in us are infinite: therefore that towards which they reach must be infinite, undefinably infinite, infinite beyond all imagining. Anything else than the greatest God there can be is not enough to justify humanity's groping hope for what may exist.

Jesus says, "Whoever has seen me has seen the Father."[1]

Ah, friends! How glorious, how radiant, how sublime this truth is! We approach it hesitatingly, only because we are afraid it may not be true. We fear to hope too high, lest the real God be found to disappoint. But can we

---

1. John 14:9

The Reflection

hope too much in God, beloved? Never. Let us therefore boldly approach the throne of grace. Our Lord says that if we have seen him, we have seen the Father. If then we have seen Christ weeping, we have seen God. If we have seen him laughing or sleeping or loving or wondering, we have seen God. If, beloved, we have seen him suffering and dying, yea, and rising again, we have seen God. If we have seen the humanity of Jesus, we have seen the face of God. The human heart of Jesus, his emotions, his conscious feeling, his will, his wishes and desires: to know these things, is for us to know the divinely human. The apostle says that through Christ, God made the world. This means that the world is made through a principle of humanity, yea, through very human heart and soul itself. The humanity of Christ—therefore humanity essential and all-participating—is the way in which all humans relate to and approach their creator. Thus, to be fully human in Christ is to be one with the eternal.

I ask the honest seeker after Christ's way with humanity, what would the heart of Christ think of a soul who was eternally lost, eternally at enmity with the source from which it came, eternally miserable and tormented? If Christ would be moved to grief, would that not mean that God's heart would be so moved also? There can be no disunity between the will of the Son and the will of the Father. The two must will the same.

Would Christ deny his own love of and brotherhood with the lost—would he crucify it—for a divine will which did not care that there were any lost at all? Christ then would be the most pitied, most suffering man! He would wish to save his kindred, yet must sacrifice love of brother and sister to keep his love of Father! Is Christ's heart eternally so crucified? What hope then have we of heaven, if there we shall be united to him? Shall heaven be mingled with such unspeakable sorrow, greatest of all in the greatest heart himself: the heart of the Son of Man?

Or does the heart of Jesus eventually cool, eventually *accept*—a horrid word—that will of God which does not reach out savingly to all men and women? Shall the love Christ had for the lost be such as to become as if it never were, as if he never loved them? Shall he grow to look upon his former love and sorrow as things of insignificance? Will Jesus become *apathetic* towards any lost human being? Weak love, were it so! May we be spared such an affection!

Or shall the heart of Christ begin to beat with a love that *rejoices* in the very lostness of the lost? Will he and his righteous saints *enjoy* the suffering, the separation, the loneliness, the rebellion of those who will never have the only thing that could reconcile their soul and give them peace? Who that has ever known the face of love, or even caught a glimpse of her garment, could believe she could even *suggest* such a countenance?

I ask my reader: did the human heart and will of Christ pray for the salvation of all humanity? If he did not, then we must look for another savior. For we need one who loves us, who sees in us at least some brotherhood, some image of the divine light, however dimly it may shine! If Christ loves us only by a command of the Omnipotent, then he has no real love towards us as objects of love, as things actually worth loving. He has a love only for the command—none for those who benefit from it. Had the command been otherwise, so too would have the affection and the friendship, the shepherding and the compassion, the sacrifice and the resurrection. But then there is nothing in us which on its own is worthy of Christ's love. There is no true blood kinship, no true connection of he and us to his Father, no real reflection in us of the divine. Can Jesus not give his heart to us *naturally*? Must he be *commanded* to do so?

How could Christ be truly human, if he, in sharing our nature, did not also naturally love those who were his kindred? What does an additional divine command impose upon the human nature of Jesus, regarding his love of his own race, which he did not already have simply by being human himself? Is there absolutely nothing in us intrinsically worthy of Christ's love? Does nothing in us call it forth? What then are we: mere potshards, indifferent to perfection or destruction? If we are not worth bringing out of our weakness, why were we brought into being? Why ought we be delivered, if our deliverance is as insignificant as our abolition? Why should we yearn to be saved, or desire that our loves ones be, since humanity is nothing more than an arbitrary placeholder, becoming valuable only supposing that God happens to declare it, the declaration itself changing nothing *about* us, but only what we are *called*?

I ask, could God have sent Christ into the world to save no one? Or to save other than those he has saved? How then does Christ *truly* love those he saves, since that love lives and is rooted in a mere conditional? How is his love towards his brothers and sisters not accidental, inconsequential? Is not the person saved a contingency that would make no difference to him were God to will differently, which he just as easily could have? What spouse would be satisfied if her husband loved her only because he was commanded? And what husband who loved his bride would ever be content if she believed such? Are we not all the bride of Christ?

"Christ's death made salvation possible. Were it not for his death, which need not have occurred, we would all be worthy of eternal separation from God."

How can that which was impossible beforehand *become* possible? If we *became* capable of salvation when Christ died, we were, already before that death, *able* to be saved. If therefore Christ's death made salvation possible, salvation must have already been possible beforehand, else it could never have become so.

"What then did Christ's death save us from, if not from an objective depravity that deserved eternal destruction?"

I say, the death of Christ saved us from a picture of God in which our eternal death was ever even imaginable. It saved us from the very thought that we *were* intrinsically worthless, that God *could* be anything other than our Infinitely Concerned Father. The death of Jesus showed us that all human beings are essentially valuable, and that they cannot *not be*. How absurd to think, that that which is necessarily worthless could *become* worthy! For then it was possible beforehand that it be worth something, in which case it was not necessarily worthless!

It is not difficult to believe that I as an individual am worth little. Such a thought can be and often is the first step on the path to humility and freedom—though, if it is not checked by a healthy awareness of one's own value, it can lead to soul-darkness and death. Yet instead of asking, "Am I worth anything?" ask, "Is my wife worth anything; is my son or daughter; is my friend?" The value we easily deny of ourselves we cannot so easily deny of others. And thank God! May we never *truly* believe the logical consequences of total depravity!

I return now to a question I began but did not complete earlier. Did Christ pray for the salvation of all? If he did not, he is no true human, since he does not care for an essential piece of himself, a fellow human being, sharing his nature. Yet if Christ did pray for the salvation of all because he truly loved all humanity out of pure and natural heart, then, I ask, was his prayer heard? And if it was heard, how could the Father who was listening, being at perfect unity of will with his Son, not grant his prayer? Is not the unity of the Father and Son the strongest, greatest thing in existence? Is not the very essence of the Father to give his divine *yes* to the Son, who asks of him what he will?

Do not busy thyself with trying to *prove* the relation between Father and Son, friend. The thing is too big to prove, like all great, infinitely meaningful things. Such things escape us from their infinity; their *simplicity* prevents them being grasped in complex thought or word. Being things of the spirit, they always outstretch the mind's ability to capture, to wrap around, to comprehend. Therefore they are eternally thinkable: existing in forms innumerable, stories uncountable, experiences never-ending, life ever-growing.

Many a philosopher will tell you that he cannot prove that the world exists, and not a few metaphysicians will disprove the existence of themselves. Is it therefore any wonder that we cannot prove the existence of our God? And what does it even mean, "to prove"? How could *we*, who come from the world—the world itself being prior to us—ever turn back around and grasp the whole thing such as to *prove* any of it? All our thinking is, as it were, borrowed from something more primal than ourselves. Thought puts the world into the soul. But to do this, it must take from the givenness of the world. How then can thought tell that *givenness* what to do or how to be? Before proving anything, everything must be assumed. Before you ever thought a thing, could you prove it? Before you saw color, before you heard music, or fell in love, or tasted an orange, or smelled the grass—could you prove these things? Why, you cannot even prove the most common thing in the world: the light by which you see, nearly every moment of your conscious existence! Examine what "light" is, and the thing falls to pieces. Proof is such a poor, starved notion of understanding, of knowing, of being! One can only prove what one already understands: therefore what he has already experienced—what he already knows!

Yet though we could never prove God or the Incarnation, I would go so far as to say that if it is not true that God is perfectly and infinitely beautiful, and if this God did not reveal himself as an absolutely perfect human love, living and dying and entering into new life, it is a lie I shall die believing. For it is the only thought that makes life worth living. If I am to believe in God and humanity, why not believe in something as high and grand as this? Such is the only notion worthy of Christian faith and hope. All else is inadequate. All else but goes begging after something grander, itself in need, itself presenting paltry things not great enough to satisfy our infinite want. Only the perfect Parenthood of God, and therefore the perfect son and daughtership of us his children, will fill our souls to the measure in which they can be filled, and therefore *must* be filled.

This faith in our human destiny is rooted in the Savior, who often spoke in similar words of the blessed necessity of our relation to the divine.

May we keep alive in our hearts the hope for our homeland, where we shall dwell forever with the One Love, of whom the apostle said, "For us there is one God, the Father, from whom are all things."

5

One God, the Father

"Indeed, even though there may be so-called gods in heaven or on earth—as in fact there are many gods and many lords—yet for us there is one God, the Father, from whom are all things and for whom we exist."

1 Corinthians 8:5–6

We see in the creation instances of an incomplete relating love, yet we hold by faith that there is One Love that is all-complete and all-sufficing. Such must be, we believe, our one God, the Father.

The thought that we are the offspring of God, and that in him we live, move, and have our being, is the most hopeful, beautiful thought that can ever enter human mind. Though one rolls it through the chamber of his heart as the ages expand to infinity, he shall never exhaust it. The relation between Maker and made, between infinite fecundity and finite expression, is bottomless, and must be, for all eternity. If we should ever reach the end of it, it would be less than it is. Like a divine rose-mystery, the more the soul looks into it, the more wonderfully expansive, the more harmoniously rich, the more warmly secret he finds it. To think that we are children of the Infinite God! To think that in him we live, and move, and have our being! It sends spirit-pulses of life to our very core, and touches our own divinity..

The creation we see reflects but does not exhaust the Divine. Is there not some whisper we can trust? Although we cannot hear clearly enough to make it out in full, we believe—oh God, we hope—that we will hear it one day as clearly as the trumpet of the archangel, and so find our home with thee.

What notion do we have of creation? We can, it seems, form no conception of an *absolutely* creative act. Where we simply rearrange already existing things, God makes the very things themselves. Where humanity puts together its novels and paintings out of bits of words and colors, God creates human beings who are themselves the living characters in his stories and works. We would make a Frankenstein, sewing together dead flesh and bone. God would make an Adam, who is himself a living soul, an unrepeatable: a *thing* itself.

All puzzles relating to God's predestination and humanity's freedom would be resolved if we but had a proper notion of what it means for God to create. The closer we attain to the truth of the notion, the closer, too, we shall get to understanding the relations between God and humanity. Every contradiction arises from not yet having a thought large enough to encompass both truths.. All notions of God, however seemingly contradictory and however primitive, have in them some truth. No disciple of Christ should forget that Christ himself grew up worshiping a God who would be to many theologians far too anthropomorphic. And yet it was this same God of the Jews who pronounced to a nation almost illiterate, that which the profoundest metaphysician can barely catch glimpse of: that his name is I AM.

Regarding notions of God, there is the finite God who, having once made the world, now stands back and allows it to evolve haphazardly. While the idea honors the fact that God has, so to speak, thrown the world off himself, and while it upholds the relation between God and the world, it implies that what God has made is somehow outside of his ultimate control. God must *deal with* what happens in the world; he is *faced with* the possibilities which come to be. He waits to see how, precisely, everything will unravel so he can *then decide* what to do. But where would these supposedly random possibilities come from, if not God himself? A possibility in God's creation is as accounted for as an actuality, and, therefore, as known and willed and loved. Even if God should say to himself, "I will create this thing with the possibility of going this way or that," the very *this way or that*—the very potency, the very either-or itself—would come from him. Therefore even the *possibilities* of the world's outcome must be rooted in God. How could the world go on, haphazardly or not, if not by God? Where would such potencies come from—such possible evolutions—if not from his hand and thought? Any way that a thing *may* be must *already* be grounded in the Maker. Else it would spring not from him but from something other than him. But there is no deeper root, no further explanation, than God. Thus there is no sense in which God could create and "then" deal with the world. For when God creates, the "then"—the *coming to be* in the thing he has made—has already been accounted for. Yet at the same time this does not mean that God "beforehand" decides what will happen in the world, as if, him having so determined things, now the world is "stuck" with its fate. How could a thing be "stuck" with being itself? The thing just is itself. If you say it "must" be what it is, that is simply a tautology, not a statement about how something other than the thing itself *forces* it to be what it otherwise could or would be. What other would-be would there be, if the created thing would not be itself? We are not, so to speak, *cast* for certain roles that we now *must* play in the universe. We simply are our roles. God does not think *about* us: he *thinks* us.

So too with all creation. God does not think about creation. He thinks creation itself. His thinking, is the world's existing. How then divide the world that God makes into the world and some imposing decree, some fixed plan, which presses upon the world and bends it to outcome x, which, without God's bending, would be have been outcome y? In truth there is and can be no *decree* that stands over an already made world and pushes upon it. Once the world is, there is already in it its own self-directed end and telos. Without God's already-bending there would not be outcome y, but nothing at all.

In creation, then, the whole outworking of the world is already posited; the world's ends are at the same time bound up with its present self. What need therefore for a decree? What purpose would it—*could* it—serve? For an all creative God, a decree is superfluous. Whatever he was trying to accomplish would already be present simply in virtue of the created product. There is no place for an *additional* coercive act, for there is nothing left over for such a thing to *do*. God's creation already entirely accounts for itself.

To think, is to imitate God, for God is essentially a thinking being. Perhaps, indeed, he is just *thinking being*, a relation of existence to itself. Therefore to think, friends, is not an evil, but a good thing. Let us see if we can think a little about creation, and get a far off glimpse of the outline of something which may throw our questions into more light.

One God, the Father

What does it mean to create? That which comes to be, before it is, is not. Yet, before it is, it somehow exists in that which makes it. The artist pre-contains his art, not in the sense that he sees his picture as it will be before he makes it, but in such a way that all the depth and harmony and beauty of what he produces is rooted in his art-soul. That which comes to be—that which the artist creates—is a finite reflection of what is in him in an infinite and therefore not totally communicable mode. Thus, to create, the artist must render his infinite into a finite. To create, he must communicate his infinite self into a finite form.

The created thing then is a certain analysis and rendering of the creator's inner, incomprehensiblelife. For this reason, creation can never exhaust the one who creates. There is always something more that is not poured into the thing made, since to make is to render finite, and to be able to make is to possess infinity. The reproductive and creative faculty is infinite, since the form of being, latent in even a human soul, dwelling deeper than the conscious self, is infinite. That is, it is a form without limitation. The creative one is like the miner who, no matter how deeply he burrows into the depths of the mountains, finds more and more gems, each unique, none repeated before. Should one be infinitely creative, he would do this infinitely, with an everlasting loveliness of richness and relation.

Creation then is a finite relation to the infinity of God. It is a participation in the divinity and incomprehensibility of existence. All created being, since it exists, is essentially and necessarily valuable, and thus what God makes *must* be good. Therefore a thing must be a perfect example of itself, for there is no other thing identical to it to which it could approximate. Everything is its own beautiful creation. There is not a better version of *you* that God could have made. For you simply are yourself: an unrepeatable individual rendition of God. So too your loved ones, so too all creatures, whether animals or atoms. Is it not wonderful to think that this is true of absolutely everything that we see? Everything is its most unique self! Nothing would be better off not existing, replaced by some better thing that could be there in its stead!

Some say God "can" create. I ask, how does this "can" attach to him? If God cannot attain some new mode of being since he is Infinite Being itself—the idea of "new mode" being the imagination's mistaken idea of some form of life which he did not previously possess and which he then goes on to acquire—how does it make sense to say God "can" do anything? What *possibility* can be attributed to the infinite *necessity*? What *potency* can enter into the all-perfect *actuality*? Can a process of *becoming* intermix with absolute *being*?

Supposing God created, would he not change? Would he not "go from" existing without a world to now existing with one? Would he not at one moment will and know only himself, and the next, will and know both himself and the world? And if so, would this not mean that he was divided? But what undivided principle would then account for and envelope such a division? And would this not be a higher principle than God himself? If God can be divided into what he could and could not be, would there not be some law above God, some larger definition of God-possibility, which gave him the potential ranges of his own existence? Would there not be, in effect, some bigger, more infinite God?

If God could go from existing *alone* to now existing *with*, would it not mean that he attained some new mode of being—whether that be in will or knowledge or relation—and that he was before limited and less than all he could be? Where would such a previous limitation come from? How could his *old-finite, old-definiteness* transform into some *new-finite, new-definiteness,* and what infinite would subsume these two finites? Would not such a subsuming, self-subsisting infinite itself be God?

"In the beginning was the Word, and the Word was with God, and the Word was God."[1] Friends, how glorious to say these words of the Gospel writer, how wonderful to think upon them! For they mean simply this: we are necessarily in the Father, for the Father necessarily has his Word, and his Word necessarily contains all creation. Be gone with the metaphysics that say that God could still be God and not know, not have in his bosom, not be the Father of his creation! Insofar as God knows his Word, he cannot but know all that is contained in his Word, yea, all that his Word could contain, in any conceivable universe!

The Father begets his Word, within which the infinite is analyzed and refracted into an infinity of finite forms. All these the Father loves and eternally breathes out and interpenetrates with his Spirit. The Word abides perfectly in the Father. It is his offspring, his conception of himself. Therefore it is one with him. Therefore all that is in this Word must be one with him as well. In uttering his Word, the creation, which is the Father's myriad and emptied out reflections of himself, comes to be. The Father therefore is the all in all that has his Word. Because of this, he knows—he must know—the unique word of every created thing.

1. John 1:1

One God, the Father

God accounts for every creature so utterly and absolutely that there is no act, no thought, no feeling, no potency which could even possibly negate the divine relation, our essential connection with him. You cannot even imagine a universe in which the created was severed from the Creator, or where it was unknown to him. St. John said that what was made *in* him—that is, in God himself—was life. We are living. Therefore we could not even in principle exist independently of God. How could a thing exist without God? Where would it be to be, if not in him? What would it be related to? Rather, as God's own offspring, we exist, every moment, in unity with him too profound for speech and thought. Words are too poor, too small, to describe the relation between us and God. It is so infinitely grand and all-encompassing that to even speak of it is already to limit it and make it less than it is. What can we do but stammer at the mystery of the infinite love in which—by which —we *are*?

"God therefore needs the creation. Do you say that God creates out of necessity?"

Does God need himself; does he need his Word? Verily. Yet the Word contains creation. If you think not actually because you think that God need not create, then still the Word contains creation potentially. If you say God need not have created, still you must hold that, he could have created if he had not. Thus, in either case, necessarily, the Word possesses creation, for the Word is related to creation as being that in which the possibility of creation is grounded. Even if creation does not exist, the Word would still know that *creation could have been*. God's Word still knows every soul that *could have* thought or breathed or loved, and this necessarily. Therefore creation—its idea and nature and being—still exists in the mind of God, necessarily. It is an essential *relata* of his thought. God cannot un-know it; his Word cannot *un-have* all worlds. Insofar as God must have his Word, therefore so too must he have in his bosom all things that could ever be.

However, to speak of God with needs is to suppose that there is some possible reality outside him that he stands over against which he can *begin* to assimilate into himself. How can the eternal fullness, the Infinite Being, the fount of all goodness and love—*attain*? All that is, all that can be, is already contained by him. He stands in no position of potency; he does not *become*. Therefore to speak of him doing something out of necessity has no place, as if his action is conceived as first being open to alternatives.

I say, God must be God; therefore he must exist, and contain in himself all that makes him God. This includes creation, and his relation to the world. But it does not follow that God is forced to do or be what he is, since "forced" is but a metaphor describing that which comes to be in time. Thus, if I must use words, I say that God must create. But not because he first stands in potency towards what he afterwards acquires; but because he must be himself—he must be a Word-having God—and already contain in himself what he is and therefore must be.

What is God without creation? Is God necessarily God? But who then is he God to? But if God is necessarily God, he must necessarily have creation. This is not a necessity that *comes* to be: it is one that simply *is*. It is the same necessity as the necessity of goodness, of life, of joy. In God there is only timeless, self-diffusive abundance. I have heard one thinker call it playfulness. Ah, friend, can we learn to look upon our God as the Divine Play?

I do not think it possible for God to know a creature and not love it, nor will its existence: for all these things in God are one. His knowing creatures is his loving them which is his willing their existence—which is just himself. Creation therefore is an eternal, necessary, essential relation existing in God himself, between his infinite self and his finite selves which he loves.

"What of God's life in himself? Can he not exist satisfied in himself, without creation?"

What does it mean to say that God exists purely "in himself"? If purely in himself, therefore neither in my mind nor words, the very mind and words which just declared that he existed purely in himself! To exist altogether in oneself, absolutely detached and unrelated, is an absurdity, an unmeaning: for all existence is relation, at the very least to the mind postulating it. To speak of God at all—to affirm anything at all about him, even his existence—is to straightway posit the speaker, the human mind, which relates to the object spoken of. You cannot posit God without the human thinker who is himself at that moment thinking "God." For the thought itself requires and depends on the mind thinking it in order to be. "God" as thought by man therefore requires man to exist. Every description at once assumes both the description and the describer, the relator and the related. Therefore description necessarily implies relation. If we affirm the existence of God at all, for that very reason we cannot say he is unrelated to us. Nothing therefore is knowable, nor can anything be said of something existing *absolutely* in itself. The phrase is an unmeaning; it conveys no idea whatever.

How many thinkers call themselves Christian but read Aristotle more than Christ! Would that they read Plato instead. If God's being a Creator is contingent, why then does God exist as Creator rather than not? Nothing in God explains why. For if the thing in God did serve as an explanation, this thing is either necessary or contingent. If necessary, once you posit it, God's being Creator would likewise follow, since if a cause is necessary, so is its effect. If the thing is contingent however, why suppose it exists? What causes the contingency of God's creating? If you posit the necessity of God, then the contingent thing would necessarily follow. Unless you said that God could be identical whether or not he caused the world. But if a necessary cause need not give rise to a necessary effect, how is the effect accounted for? Why is the cause then called a cause? How could the world exist, if God causing the world is identical to his not causing it?

"God is essentially omnipotent. His omnipotence is his ability to bring about an effect. Therefore, God's being omnipotent explains the effect of the world and why it exists."

Yet, if God is not *essentially* Creator, then neither need omnipotence be an *essential* attribute of his, and for the same reason. For if power in God means the ability to bring about an effect, then God would be God—that is, he would have an essential attribute and relation— in virtue of his bringing about the world. But then, God would be God in his being a cause of the world, in which case he *would* be essentially Creator.

"But God need not bring about the world. Therefore, his omnipotence consists not in the world as actually existing, but only in its being able to exist."

Yet this still means that God is essentially denominated by his ability or reference towards another. Therefore God must be essentially constituted by his relation to this other. That is, God must be essentially related to the world, if he is essentially omnipotent. But then he must essentially be its cause: he could not be God unless he were its cause. In a word, God could not be God unless he was *essentially* God to the world. He must, then, in the essential necessity of his being, be its Father. He cannot be anything else and still be God.

This point applies to *all* the divine attributes which have the world as referents: power, wisdom, knowledge, etc. For just what is God knowledgeable and wise and powerful *about*? Do you say the world? Then I ask: is the world essential to God? If not, then neither can he be essentially powerful, wise, and knowledgeable, for these are mere contingencies which do not define his essence. If the world is not essential to God, then neither is God's knowledge of the world, his power, or his wisdom essential to him. Where then is our Christian God, if you take away his mind and will, and make them mere logical relations of *our* mind?

Do all these arguments frighten you, friend? Do they make your God feel remote or like a mystery unapproachable? Verily God would be such, were he not essentially Father. Make this unto thee a new commandment: thou shalt not let the consequences of a metaphysical argument destroy thy faith in the redeemer of man. May we all be strong and courageous in the face of the mystery of existence! If our hearts condemn us, and if they tremble at the awful obscurity of the infinite, I say, let us worship till our last breath a God of all-beauty and all-relation, a God who is his own perfect life in his very being our Father.

Therefore like the angel bearing tidings of good news, I cry, do not be afraid! Do we not believe that God has given us his Son? And has not his Son told us that God is our Father? Has he not shown us that we are such that he would die for us? How therefore can we fear God, if we are so meaningful to Jesus? We may not understand it, but still, Christ died for us and said that if we trust in him, he will save us from every nihilism and confusion that lurks in human heart or brain. Christ told us that if we believe in him, we will be one with the Father, as he himself is one with the Father. Let us then try to be one with our Lord!

Do you think that there could be a human being to whom God was not a Father? Verily, it cannot be. Where would the fatherless come from, if not God? Where would such a spark originate, if not the light that lighteth everyone? Did not St. Paul say that, for us there is one God, the Father, *from whom* are *all* things? All humans, then, and sinners too, and lost souls, and all who wonder far from truth, yea, any possible being in any thinkable universe, any creature that could ever want or feel or reason or have the faintest conscious sensation of faith or hope or joy: to all such, God is—must be—a Father. Oh kindred spirit! The one blessed fact in existence is this: *our God must be the universal Parent of us all.* He cannot but be, for all things come from him, and in his Son he knits together all humanity.

Ah, do not forget the words of Jesus when he said, towards those who would not forgive their neighbor, that so too *their* Father would not forgive them. See then how, even in the warning, there is couched the necessity of the Fatherhood. See then how God is even Father to those who, at the time, he does not forgive, because they do not forgive, and so do not enter into their own forgiveness. See then how, even when God does not forgive, it is to his *child* that he withholds forgiveness! Behold how grandly, how infinitely God is Father, even to the wicked and unforgiving! Truly if God is Father to these, he is Father to all!

And if he is not Father to the unjust—that is, to sinners—who was he a Father to before Christ came, before Christ died? Who was God a Father to when the apostle said, "God proves his love for us in that *while we still were sinners* Christ died for us"?[2] Verily, he is Father to sinners beforehand, before they know themselves his children! Therefore he is a Father to all, even if they know it not.

Do you say that God merely adopted us as children when Christ came? Do you say that we *become* his children only at the moment he imputes the blood of Christ's sacrifice to us, and that before this we are aliens and orphans? Do you believe that we have no natural sonship in us from our creation, from the first?

How many say that we are not *naturally* children of God, but that we only *become* such when he makes us so! Until then, they say, we are "by nature sinners" who *deserve* eternal punishment. I ask, what does the word "naturally" mean when talking about the relation between Maker and made, between creature and Creator? What we are naturally, we cannot help being; indeed we must be, because God made us so. Yet if I am not naturally God's child, how am I naturally a sinner? How is God in either case not altogether responsible for my whole being, sinner or no? And if God is in either case responsible, how am I not in either case his child? How is he not in either case my Father? I ask, how does God not stand in a necessary and inviolable relation of Fatherhood to all men and women that he brings into the world, from the very moment they begin to be, in the absolute totality of their existence? How were we, aliens and unnatural bastards, *able* to be adopted before God adopted us, if we were not naturally children of his? That which *may be* a son, *already* stands in potency towards sonship. There is therefore sonship necessarily latent, in germ. From the very nature of the case, then, a natural childhood must exist in all who Christ *can* die for, and Christ can—indeed *has*—died for all. We cannot then be natural aliens from the Source from which we came. We must be *necessarily* related to God. We must *naturally* be able to be assimilated into him harmoniously.

2. Rom 5:8

Surely God made all humans beings. Yet if this is so, God made even sinners—even they are connected to him as things created from the Creator, as thinking and feeling beings sprung from his mind and will. Therefore no matter how wicked they become, they must still be *able* to be more than what they now are, else God could never save them. But if one can grow closer to the heart of his God, he cannot be naturally worthless. The mere fact that our God can grow in us is proof against our nihilism. There is a God-spark in us all, else we could not be, could not exist, could not think or love or feel any goodness at all. This divine light in us is the contact of the soul with its Source. Our nature then cannot be antithetical to God's nature, as that which is totally other and worthless and incapable of goodness; it cannot be totally depraved, else we could never approach or reflect God, could never be united to Christ and be at one with the Father. Our salvation would, in principle, not even be possible. You say one cannot be a child of God unless God takes the evil person that is there and makes him a child. But how did the evil one get there in the first place? Was he not created by God? What then is God taking and molding, except that which he already made, already endowed with potencies and powers towards a future evolutionary oneness with himself? If God takes a heart of stone and turns it into a heart of flesh, it is only because the heart of stone already had within it the ability to be turned into a heart of flesh. And it could only have this if God created it so.

Even if you say that God did not create the natural depravity of all who have fallen after Adam, he at least made the system that gave rise to this fact. For who made it that sin and therefore separation and therefore total depravity and damnation or annihilation, who made it that these were possible, and that such a chain of effects ensued from some cause? Who or what grounds the ghastly fate—that the sin of one should lead to such a consequence, where all who come after have no hope of salvation, unless God lifts them indifferently out of their necessity towards evil? Whoever made such a—whoever gave it live utterance—commands the impossible, and punishes that which he has purposefully willed into existence. Surely no child of Adam willed to be born a natural sinner. Who then did? Before Adam's offspring is born who shall be under Adam's curse, who is God angry with? Adam? Is God then angry with *Adam* for bringing into existence sinful creatures, and does he then willingly punish the *offspring* who cannot but do what Adam destined them to do, based on his own decree? Is God now wrathful that a depravity exists which does so because he decreed it? With such absurdities, is it any wonder that unbelief exists?

Or does God not will the corruption at all, but tolerate it with heavy heart? And yet if so, why does he go on damning those who cannot repent? How can God *tolerate* that which he has *purposefully* created, which cannot be other than his predestining? Is God unhappy with what he has himself brought about? Or is there some condition—some chain of cause and effect—which exists independently of his creative intention, that he is eternally confronted with, which is forever clawing at his heart? If the possibility of damnation was not made and intended by God, and if it is something he does not wish, then of all hearts of love God's himself is the most pitied—for he cannot help it that billions upon billions come into existence and may be lost to him forever! For all he knows and can control, every soul he makes may be destined to eternal ruin! Poor denizen of torment, unable to deliver himself or his children: a God with no God to save himself from himself; a God bound by the metaphysical chains he eternally finds himself with! Is there a thought more terrible?

The potential for eternal punishment was either intended by God, or it was not. If it was, he must have positively willed the hideous outcome, at least as a possibility for some. It may be, as some say, on certain grounds having to do with things outside his control, such as creaturely freedom. I will not now speak about the strangeness in supposing that a God of love could create a type of freedom which could possibly lead to its own destruction, seeing as that same God would have to decide just how many wicked choices would result in a state of *irrevocable* solidification in evil, and therefore damnation. I will only say that even such a metaphysic of freedom, with such a combination of sins and their subsequent hardening effects, are still limits Almighty Love himself has laid down. Such limits have still sprang from *his* loving hand which *he* finds tolerable. The whole dilemma is this: *the whole human condition, whatever it is, comes from God.*

In the end, all reasons to justify the eternal damnation of a human soul amount to the same: God either intends, or suffers, the ultimate destruction of his creation, beings which he has made of his own choice, in his own image, with the potential for infinite happiness. For my part, I cannot tolerate either. For then I cannot love my God, or I pity him beyond words.

Surely no one shall say that there are some souls that God is not *able* to make his children. But then none stand outside his omnipotent loving will. All then must have in them germs of sonship and daughtership. Since

Ears of Corn

God shall not fail in reconciling all to himself, since he wills all to be saved, and since the one Elder Brother Jesus will one day deliver the whole human kingdom—yea, and all heaven and earth—into the hands of the Father, can we not trust that all men and women shall be brought into their pure childlike relation to the source from which they came? If God can do it, he surely shall, since he is Father, and since he is good. If he cannot do it, then we did not come completely from him; we were not born entire of his heart and thought. There stands an eternal inability in us, an implacable obstacle he is faced with that he cannot overcome, that he did not create. Where could this evil come from, now loose in creation, with all the metaphysically *real* powers that only goodness can have? Resistance, defiance, love of self, self-will. These are essentially good. How then can evil have final sway over them? How can evil so fully corrupt them that they can go on living forever in their corrupted form? Is not life stronger than death, and good greater than evil? It must be, if there is a good and evil, that evil is weaker than good, and that the good in each creature will one day eradicate the evil.

Thank God, brothers and sisters, that we did come from God! And thank God that we have a Father! If this one thing be true, what better news could there be? What grander reality can be imagined than to be utterly derived from an omnipotent love, who holds us in his bosom as a child? Ah, friends! If we cannot believe it, let us hope for it with all our might!

Jesus never once told us that some system made us one with God: but that he—the Son—did. That is, that man there, Jesus Christ, doing the will of the Father, tells us that if we do as he did, and think as he thought, we can, yea, we will, like him, be one with the source from which we came, and have eternal life. We can either do as Jesus did and look up with our hearts and cry to God as *Abba*, or not. I shall not judge one who shall not try. But for my part, if I did not at least try to believe that the Infinite One out of which I came was altogether my Father—yea, and my mother and friend and lover and my utter All in All—why, if I did not at least try to seek the hidden face of my God, I know not why I should live.

Yet while we are in this vale, our living towards our God is plagued by sin, for, as the apostle said, "Through one man, death came through sin, and so death spread to all men because all men sinned."

6

As Sin Came into the World

"Therefore, just as sin came into the world through one man, and death came through sin, and so death spread to all because all have sinned."

ROMANS 5:12

WHAT THE APOSTLE MEANT when he wrote these words, what images of death flitted through his mind, or what metaphysical implications he supposed he was conveying, are questions which, I believe, we shall never answer in this world. Some spend years studying what this or that thinker believed about Paul's words here. Thus we have schools of what this or that theologian taught and how such teaching fits into a system, with its various cogs and wheels. I do not see Paul in this passage, or for that matter, very often at all, trying to create a definite *system*, except insofar as his systematizing means to preach Christ crucified. Indeed if Paul did mean to teach a set of abstract propositions, I think it no disrespect to say, his writing would have been a good deal more systematic.

As if a set of syllogisms, pegged up on the classroom board of the mind, could give life! Could we make a system out of life? How could we form compartments tight enough to prevent the Spirit of God from seeping through and interpenetrating every thought, every proposition, every category that we had? Nothing but the living, working, humanity of Christ in us can give life, and if we are not in the kind of vital relation to God

Ears of Corn

as Jesus was with his Father, no collection of *points* could suffice to communicate such a thing essential. Words are poor, stunted things, hemmed and cramped by the necessity of their finitude. When the richer medium of *thought* is forced to present itself in the smaller medium of *word*, *word* cannot but misrepresent *thought*. At the best, *word* hopes to avoid mistake. At the worst, it belies grossest distortion.

To know what another thinks or teaches about St. Paul's words is, in one respect, very important. For insofar as another may see the truth in Paul's writings that we cannot see, that other can help us. Yet it is of the utmost necessity to remember that our main task in reading others' commentaries on the apostle is not to listen to these others themselves—nor is our main task even to listen to Paul—but to listen to the *truth* in each. What good would it do to know what Luther or Aquinas thought *about* what Paul said, if that *truth* which Paul was straining to convey, and which we were, in our inner being, yearning after, remained altogether hidden from us? Christ is the one human truth, and he came to give this to us. That is, he came to give us himself. His spirit working in us is our life. It is only insofar as we are drawing the truth of his humanity into our hearts, that reading the words of Paul or any other thinker are any good to us.

Before any think I am disparaging Paul I would ask him to consider whether the apostle himself would have agreed with me. Would not he have thought that our allegiance was first and foremost to Christ, and only to another thinker, even if that thinker were himself, insofar as he conforms to the Son? Would Paul not have said, nay, insisted that, if we could not understand his words, or if we thought, after much thinking, that he spoke something untrue, would not Paul himself implore us to follow the truth as we saw it, rather than deny our conscience and believe him? I think Paul would have said to all who would be honest disciples of Christ: "Follow Paul, follow Apollos, follow Cephas, but only insofar as each follows truth. For is truth divided? Therefore, if any seem to depart—even myself or an angel from heaven—hold fast to what truth you have attained. For that is what we are straining after also. God will reveal unto all even what they need to know."

If then we cannot see the truth in some Christian theologian, though he shows us what seem the logical deductions of the words Paul or Christ, we cannot believe his teaching. This is because, by taking up that theologian's words, the truth we saw becomes untrue. We see the chain of reasoning and adopt his system, but a fog falls over our vision of Christ, and the blessed flame of truth flickers out. How can one say he believes a thing which, to all his honest thinking, appears to him either unintelligible, or false? Our hearts cannot beat of themselves if they bear another's rhythm. They need and have, like all hearts, their own. Nor can we feel as truly ours what only another feels as truly his.

Two thinkers may be walking truly, though they disagree on the same propositions. I do not say that there is no thing as truth, nor that we cannot share it, nor that we cannot trust our fellow human unless we see a thing ourselves. I only say, unless we feel the truth ringing in our ears, no lie will bring its music into us. Unless we feel the truth of the truth itself, at best it becomes a second-hand thing, not truly our own, and the light that is in us darkens. And verily, it grows darker still the more we try to call it light.

Oh friends, we must speak of what we know! We must tell of what we see! I desire beyond utterance a complete synthesis of feeling and thought: between what *is* and what *seems*, between psychological experience and metaphysical fact. But until we see clearly, if all we can say is "I do not presently see the truth, but, whatever it is, it cannot be *that*," then that is all we must say. Else we call one Savior who does not seem, in our heart of hearts, to be true Savior himself.

It is with this in mind that I turn to the words of the apostle. I do not turn to what some current system of theology holds to be his meaning. I turn to a way of reading his words, from which I draw life. As for what *precisely* St. Paul meant—that is, what the literal fruition of his own thought-form was when he wrote—I shall let Paul himself say. Since he uttered the riddle, he should explain it. This, I believe, all honest thinkers should concede when they approach words of another thinker that they cannot fully understand.

How I read Paul here, how I interpret his words with the grammar of my own experience of existing in God's world, is this. Sin, and its consequent evils and sufferings, once injected into the human race, must of necessity reverberate back into it in its entirety. This is because humanity is one: a giant organism, spread through time. When one part suffers, the whole suffers also. The non-human creation gives but a wider example of this. The universe, wherein humanity lives and breathes and has its being, is a lovely, divine family-gathering of relation and existence, wherein everything, from smallest atom to largest galaxy, is affected and impacted by everything else. Thus, once sin enters, it must, of necessity, spread to all; it must touch all. I do not say it must impact all the same. The sin of angels no doubt has far different consequences than those of men and women; and those of men and women than those of beasts. What degree *conscious suffering* goes up and down the chain, I cannot tell. My point is simply that, once the first pain of evil has cried out in the first suffering soul in the universe, it must reverberate to all who are themselves able to cry. Since the consequences of sin must necessarily be hideous—for if they were not, why call sin evil, and how differentiate it from good?—these consequences must be felt more profoundly by those with more profoundly loving hearts. I believe the Son of Man hung upon the cross for this very principle of unity.

To speculate, therefore, on whether the apostle here meant physical death when referencing the consequences of the first sin, or spiritual, or at one place in the text physical, and another spiritual, playing on the distinction between the flesh and the spirit, as he was wont to do, is but a trifle. It would not affect his argument whether physical death occurred before the sin of Adam. For I can well imagine a death spread across the whole earth for millions of years that was nonetheless a joy beyond words to the consciousness that freely yielded it. It is pain and evil—that is, it is *suffering*—which Paul's argument touches upon, not the mere cessation of one form of life.

The desire before sin arrives is the desire to *have* and is itself good. This desire meets both the true self in the creature and the false self: the courageous, expanding, grand self, and the fearful, tribal, small self: the God-self and the human-self. There is thus a fork in the road. The choosing self must make a claim to one side, must assert itself in one direction: either for the lower self or the higher. It is only by choosing the lesser good of keeping itself, rather than giving itself, that the desire of keeping itself swells to an unhealthy proportion. The potency towards the distortion beforehand was not evil. What is more, without the whole conflict before the person—without the person knowing itself as housing the very battlefield between the small and great selves—could it even know itself as a self, with a God above it? How know you are, and God is, unless you know both self and God? What is a human soul if not that which, once it becomes aware of itself as *I*, now enters into battle with itself—whether it will give itself or keep itself? Who knows the depth of power in such a conflict, towards both evil and good! The death that reigns in us all from the sin of Adam is but a figure of the death that reigns in all creation—yea, in Christ himself— which sprang from the first sin of Satan, or whatever creature who first said

"I" and resisted the divine urging of God. And yet all is a seed that gives rise to the resurrection.

The apostle speaks of the first sin bringing *condemnation* to all. He speaks of the free act of Adam as constituting in his progeny a state of trespass, a state of being "made sinners." Does he mean, as some say he does, that, since Adam sinned, now all humans ever born, even before their birth, are under a necessary condemnation to eternal hell? Does Paul mean that no soul has any choice but to follow its wicked and hellish desires into the flames—the desires themselves being decreed by Adam's sin—with its teeth barred in hatred of God? I ask, does Paul here mean to say—*saint* Paul, who wept over the separation of his brothers from Christ, and wished to be accursed for their sake—does he mean to imply that eternal suffering awaits all humans ever born for a crime they did not commit, or for crimes that they cannot of themselves stop from committing, unless God chooses to graciously deliver them? If Paul did mean this, ought he not have plainly said so? Should he not, at least, have been as clear as I was just now? For such a world-shattering claim, a claim that subverts the very nature of God and humanity, Paul ought to have taken as great pains as he could to be as clear as possible. He ought to have said, "Some children will suffer unimaginable torment for all eternity for the sin of Adam." Surely if Paul believed such a doctrine, he would, somewhere, have given us such a sentence! If he believed it—if he *knew* it was true—surely Paul would have spelled it out as clearly as any five point acronym, invented fifteen hundred years later!

"Unless God gives us grace, all offspring of Adam are under the wrath of God, and doomed to eternal pain."

Wherefore call it grace, since the very God who grants it is the one who established the necessity which requires it? And wherefore call it wrath, since the one wrathful is confronted with a world he has altogether predestined? I ask, will God make creatures which cannot but hate him and then torment them for that? Ask yourself if you can honestly believe it. If you can, I leave you to the god it gives you.

"But truth is truth. It is what it is regardless of our opinions about it."

In God's universe, can the truth be anything other than all-beautiful to him who understands it? Christ said, "Let the little children come to me."[1] What truth therefore in God's creation is inappropriate for the ears of a child? Surely, of all people, it is to *our children* that we should give God's sweet truth. When a child who has lost his parent asks, "Where is my

---

1. Matt 19:14

mommy? Where is my daddy?" will you tell them that they may be lost in hellfire? Even if they *are* not, they *may be*. And there is the whole problem. For if the parent *may be* lost, the parent *may* have been expendable to the child—and God himself! The child therefore must make himself such as to view this most vital relation of his as something meaningless, something he is able to do without. I ask, how can the relation between child and parent be so weak? How can it be something even *able* to be lost, even *possibly* annihilated in human soul?

To suppose the total depravity of humanity is to suppose that God hates what he has intentionally brought about. It is to suppose that he creates things which of themselves cannot but sin and then torments them for doing what he has either made them do or knew for certain that they would do. To say that the whole predicament is due to the free sin of our first parent does nothing to remove the difficulty. It only presses on it more. For was the first sin a free act that could have been resisted? If no, then God punishes what cannot be avoided. And if the event was not avoidable by humanity, then it must have been avoidable by God, else God has faced for all eternity a metaphysical necessity—another law of being apart from himself—which he neither willed nor created: an unavoidable "first sin." On the other hand, if the first sin could have been resisted but was not, why conclude that this brought about a metaphysically necessary law whereby all souls born afterward are doomed to eternal pain? Did God leave the first sin free but then predestine all else irresistibly? Or did God create a single human pair and bestow on them the power to make God less powerful than himself, in his desire to save all humanity? Shall God make an earthly father who has more influence over the salvation of his child than God has? How could that which is made—since all its laws and consequences of action come from that which makes it—cause its Maker to be anything other than what the Maker wanted it to be? If God is truly perfectly good and loving and powerful, how could even sin change this?

Yet it does not follow that, because we are not damned forever for the sins of Adam, we nowise suffer from his sins. I take it a grand mystery, interpenetrating the relations of universe and spirit, that the acts of one can be *other than* and yet *in* the acts of another. I am not speaking of a mere legal imputation—a mere *covering* of the acts of one by the acts of another, or of a counting of what one did *as if* it were the work of another. I cast far from me the image of the dung under the snow of an imputed righteousness. In such a system, the evil of my sin is never really cleared away. The dung is still there, littering the sweet universe of God, for all eternity. It is—alas—only covered and hid! And yet from who? Surely not God, who sees all. Nor to me the sinner, who knows himself to be what he is. Precious little salvation that, which takes away neither the blot nor the one who blots: neither the sin nor the sinner! How could thirsting soul ever be truly glad in the universe of his Father, if it remained for all eternity—along with all its loved ones—the very thing it longs to be delivered from? Humanity wishes to be transformed: yet, it shall never really leave its old self behind! It shall carry its dung in its pockets always! We want *purity*. Shall we ever be pure? Will the thing we wish for *never* come to pass? I desire no presumption, friend. Lord Christ if there be any in me, cast it from me as far as the East is from the West. I do not want to be good so that I can tell myself that I am good. I want to be good so that I may *be good*. How therefore can I ever really be what I wish if my goodness is never really my own, but only that of another that I cover myself up with? Am I not still there beneath the other's clothes? And am I not still rotten, filthy, impure?

Certainly Christ came to save all from both the ancestral sin of Adam and our own personally committed sins. But the guilt from the sins we commit is very different than the state in which each of us is born. The nature that I am born with is a wonderful thing, and yet it carries with it the great burden of the self. It is therefore a nature that exists to be transcended. The simple fact that our divided nature exists at all, anywhere, is the trouble. The human condition, as it is, *ought not to be forever*. It *ought* to be transformed. It *ought* to die and be raised again. Therefore, it *must* be. May we Christians always remember this. When we argue with our fellow brother or sister, our goal is to help us both transcend the low, struggling, fearful consciousness that marks our birth into self-awareness and self-survival. How often this is forgotten! How often one becomes concerned, not with finding truth, but with being right!

The Adam living in us does not make us guilty with a guilt prior to or independent of our freely *becoming* guilty by sinning ourselves. The freely giving in, the deep *siding with* the evil and smallness in the inner self, is a thing neither conscience nor experience lets anyone deny. Whatever philosophical puzzles arise between the universality of sin's occurrence and its particularity in each sinner, the experience of *freely sinning* is a fact common to the human condition. The death in us wrought by the first sin is thus a disease of the race, a symptom of which is conscious shame, trouble, and objective condemnation: not condemnation to eternal hell, but condemnation to self, to all that is less than perfect and vital and healthy in humanity—all that is pure in thought and feeling. Such is the necessary effect on the human family of evil.

One may ask: why did God make it so that humans are able to do such evil to one another and feel so much pain? Why did he make humanity emerge in this context of selfishness and sin, where we are *able* to do evil? Why make the soul even *able* to suffer so? Why let pain even enter its consciousness? Why did God make us such as we are? Could he have done no better?

To which I say: if God did not make us what we are, who would we be? If he did not make us human, how could humans—how, therefore, could *we*—exist at all?

I believe that the universe is so woven together that should one string of its vast tapestry be disturbed, it will affect the whole cloth. That is just the way it is, because that is just what the universe is: the all-connected thing. If this fact were different, the universe would not be itself. Yet if this were *all*—if we were *simply* interrelated to everything—we might well end in despair. For if God was not great enough to bring good out of such a thing, what would be the point of our hope and belief? If I cannot trust even a human to invest my money because his uncertainty prevents him from guaranteeing a good return, how can I trust a God who made a world that ends, for all he knows and can control, in unspeakable ruin?

Brothers and sisters, if Christ is not raised from the dead, our faith is in vain. Yet thank the Father of him that he was, for by this we see both the power and love of God: power in that God *can* make all things new; love in that he *shall*. God would not have let so great an evil as sin, with such pervasive and horrible effects as the foul suffering that we see, into the universe, and, what is more, into the conscious feeling of any of his creatures, unless he could ensure for those creatures a deliverance far greater than the pains that they endured. Where sin abounds, the grace of God abounds more.

Yet I know the thought that is in the mind of not a few of my readers:

"You say that God has made us free—free to submit to him, or free to reject him. If that is so, he cannot guarantee that *anyone* will eventually be perfected and delivered from the self, let alone *all*."

You mistake. To say that God has made us free to submit or reject him here or there, or in this or that, is not to say that he has made us free to *ultimately* reject him—that is, finally and eternally, in the ultimate recesses of our being, once our freedom has had its consequences worked out and shown to us.

"Therefore, what God gives and what he is staking the whole labor and pain of the universe on accomplishing—namely, the free response of his creature, that which he cannot force by mere power—is something which, at length, he will in fact accomplish by mere power?"

No, God does not work now this way and now that, nor can he act by mere power in itself, divorced and abstracted from love and wisdom. As if God could at one time act by one part of himself out of many! The divine relation to the world is one. Therefore the freedom God gives his creatures is one. He does not "allow" and then "overpower." His allowing is but the first fruits of a kind of freedom which will eventually of itself give way to necessity—not from overpowering, but in the freest *yes* ever uttered by living soul.

"You speak in riddles and contradictions. If a man is free to come to God or not, not even God can ensure that he shall. Unless God removed the man's freedom, the very thing he gives. But that would be for God to undue what he did."

The freedom God gives is not a static kind which remains always where it began. It lives and grows and corrects itself. What was possible for it yesterday is no longer possible for it today. After so many years and experiences, who knows what it may solidify into? What God has made—yea, what he has predestined—is this very process of the fructification of freedom itself.

All freedom is a seed which begins in a *may* and flowers into a *must*. To one who denies it I ask, is there nothing you have done, which you might not have, that resulted in a repentance and hatred of the very thing that you did? In a word, has your very sinning never led you to hate the fact that you *could* so sin, and hate that fact so much that you *resolved* never to sin again? And would it not be true that, had you not ever been allowed to sin, you would never have seen how horrible your own ability to sin was in the first place, and, therefore, never formed the resolution? If so, then what you did freely and what you could have avoided led to that which you freely felt that you could not avoid: detestation of your selfish self! And thank God! Were such impossible, sin itself could never lead to life. Having once sinned and God now having no means to set us right (since he made a freedom which would lead inevitably downward in the same way that life and righteousness leads upward), the whole race would, after one sin, be led to irrevocable ruin!

To one who freely resists—that resistance will be taken up and glorified into his being for all time. It must be. How shall evil ultimately taint God's creation once that creation is fully glorified?

I often wonder, will there be a single completed state of glorification of the universe entire, or will each conscious creature itself reach a glorified state, as for all eternity God continues pouring forth more creatures who must do battle with the trial of self, and so struggle out of their chrysalis into the sweet freedom of being full creatures of God? Does our glorification in heaven entail us being free from sin, but not entail a statically completed state, but instead an ever-growing, ever-expanding consciousness of God's splendor? It is easy to imagine being free from suffering, and still continually growing in joy. Such things may my readers ponder with me to cultivate hope. Whatever the truth is, God shall see to it that our imagination does not reach higher than the reality.

For the present purpose, the point stands: what it means to be human is to be free to God's call—to be free to display bravery and follow, or to resort to cowardice and stay behind. To follow makes union with God easier and faster. It does not make union, once attained, more complete, for union is itself its own perfection. No doubt, resistance makes attaining this more difficult and delayed. And yet God shall not for that reason leave any who resist him finally outside, once and for all. No human can fully rest outside of union with God—he cannot find his end there—because that is not humanity's perfection. The human is necessarily oriented towards God. God is the light of being, which, like an infinitely present light, shines upon all that is. Nothing is where God is not. Where anything is, there too is God. The creature can turn nowhere away from God's everywhere.

There must come a time when all tongues freely and gladly confess and every knee bow to the Father. This is not through a divine overpowering. For God is not standing by, begging and pleading with humanity to come to him, only to finally, after he has ultimately failed, take away the former freedom he gave them—that which makes their coming all the more meaningful because all the more of themselves. Our freedom is not of that kind. Rather, it is very freedom itself which is organically alive, which self-corrects and builds upon itself, which enlightens and enlivens its own clarity, desire, and choosing. It is very freedom that makes itself see that it is only most free when it can no longer say no, but only yes. This is not a necessity imposed from without, not a trump card that God plays once he runs out of all his tricks, but a self-blossoming necessity from within.

Our will therefore is a self-growing revelation where, more and more, the *may* of its freedom solidifies into its own self-assented to *must*. It is like sleep. One can resist sleep freely here and there, but not forever. Eventually the soul *will* fall asleep—*freely*. For even our resisting, in the end, only serves to increase our sleepiness, and fuel what we do with sweetest necessity.

If this very thing were not true—if freedom did not lead towards its own perfection and clarity, and if it had the potential for final destruction as a counterpoise for ultimate union—this very thing must have come from God's creative hand. But how can an all good and powerful God bring forth that which has in it the potential for infinite evil? Are we to think that God *desires* such a possibility—that the creature he has given the gift of freedom to will potentially end in eternal torment or demise? Could that life which God is ever-pouring into each creature, every moment, and that which he sent his Son into the world to save, could that very gift of life become nothing more than a failed it-could-have-been? Shall the God whose heart throbs with a love unspeakably beautiful be met with a tragedy just as terrible, because of that love? Or shall God's heart finally cool to where it never really mattered that human beings existed and were lost, these children with dreams and hopes of union, with potential for joy unspeakable, which even the tongues of angels cannot declare? Shall, after ages and ages, the memory of even a single human's face, of its glorious eyes, of its childlike smile, of its heavenly potential, become insignificant to God? Or to us?

In the name of Jesus Christ, do not believe it, friend. The evil cannot, even possibly, triumph over the good. Else it would be as equal, as powerful, as full of meaning and life. If it were even *possibly* victorious, good could *possibly* be defeated. But thank God, who will have all men and women be saved, whose might cannot be overthrown by any hand, nor intentions brooked by any will: *the good shall never be defeated*. Though it can for a time be resisted, even this resistance is there only by the good's appointment. Therefore it must serve its glorious and inevitable blossoming and assimilation into very Goodness and Life itself.

"If God has predestined the good things we do, then we cannot do otherwise. Thus the freedom you prize so highly is false, and all, even evil, falls again under the fatal divine necessity. Otherwise God cannot secure his end; otherwise he can't make good his promise that all things work together for good."

How could a divine necessity from an all-beautiful God ever be *fatal*? Indeed, what could *give* life, but such a will essential?

God in creating created an all-perfect, all-loving, responsive universe for every possibility of our freedom—yea, every possibility of an infinite combination of freedoms, all interworking and intermingling. It is very Goodness itself that has decided how far our yes's and no's go. It is Love Omnipotent that has set all the limits to our freely choosing. We are free to choose what we will, not to bring to pass what we will. We are not free to make God's creative act different than it is, to undo the universe. God makes the choice up to us, but the consequences of our choices are still in his omnipotently creative hands. We feel we can control our resistance to his nudge when he allows us. Yet we feel also that we cannot even control our next conscious thought or emotion. The whole situation of our necessities and contingencies is within his all-making, therefore we can have the widest freedom, and God can still ensure that his will is *ultimately* done. For is not everything—the whole game of the universe—functioning under his wise and loving rules? Doubtless there are, at times, a better and a worse choice for us to make. Still, the fact that there is a choice between the two in the first place is an occasion that leads to its own consequential perfection. Thus, in the all-encompassing act of creation, the risk of freedom has already been weighed; it has already been calculated and accounted for. So, too, then, all sufferings have been considered. The divine creation is itself a divine *yes*—a divine *let there be*—to all that could possibly be. God has already stared in the face, taken into himself, and perfected in his own heart-plan, all worlds. How then doubt his providence? Has he not accounted for all that you *may* do with all that he *shall*?

The whole matter can be summed up in this: our freedom is still of God, from God, and rooted in God. Thus it must be destined for—it cannot escape—his glory. No end from the All-Perfect could be otherwise. My friends, the greatest truth in the world is this. God must be God. Therefore he must be to us more than we could ever hope or imagine.

It should now be obvious that to think of God as standing back arbitrarily deciding whether he shall interfere with our freedom is, I believe, a mistake. God is not picking and choosing what to do based on a whim, whereas now he is more hampered than he was a moment ago, or wishing he could do now what he did then. God is not waiting for a threshold of prayers to reach his ear which would move him to do some good he would otherwise be unable and therefore unwilling to do. All God's action is bound up in his act of creation itself, which is one. Each moment and each choice and each consequence are connected, back from the beginning of time and extending forever infinitely, as one vast interconnected web of meaning and relation.

To say that God singularly intervenes is to say that he sometimes undoes his own creating. It is to say that he sticks his finger in a universe already totally saturated with his being. Is not creation itself already adapted to bring about whatever effect would result, given so and so? Does not intervention imply that God is not already maximally responsible for the world? Does it not mean that he is somehow not all-present? If God is not present to the world, if he is not fully responsible for it, how then does it go on? If God *becomes* present when he was not, how present was he before? How would God's presence post-intervention be different from his presence pre-intervention? Did not the pre-intervened world already spring from him; was it not already made by an omniscient mind and loved by a perfect will? Did not all creation already live and move and have its being in the Living One?

"Do you not then believe in miracles?"

I ask, what is a miracle? Tell me your definition and I shall tell you what I believe. If by miracle you mean the singular intervention of God on some occasion, when he comes into a universe he was not already in, or changes the laws that he has already created, it should be plain that I do not believe in such a thing. That idea is either meaningless or contradictory. But this does not mean I do not believe in miracles. I prefer this old thinker's definition: "Whatever appears that is difficult or unusual above the hope or power of them who wonder."[2] In this sense all life to me is miraculous: the universe is saturated in miracle. For who can find *usual* the fact that he exists? Is the whole thing not magical? Why should I be ashamed to say it, or you to think it?

Magic—ah—what a grand, childlike, God-soaked word! How could the creation of the universe—and the creation of ourselves—be anything less? I ask, if almighty God's *creating* is not magical, whatever else could be? Or do you look down upon the word *magic*? I say, take heed, brother or sister, lest you rob your life of its wonder, that balm of soul which has no substitute; that medicine for innumerable spiritual diseases; that deliverance

---

2. http://www.newadvent.org/fathers/1306.htm.

from perplexities infinite. I venture to say that, even with the most learned metaphysics, even with all philosophy built upon itself from the beginning of time, humanity has not yet begun to draw the first letter in the book of God's magic.

But to return. The same person who gave this definition of miracle—no less than Augustine himself—also held that God cannot act contrary to the divinely established and universal order of things. He said,

> But God, the Author and Creator of all natures, does nothing contrary to nature; for whatever is done by Him who appoints all natural order and measure and proportion must be natural in every case . . . For we give the name nature to the usual common course of nature; and whatever God does contrary to this, we call a prodigy, or a miracle. But against the supreme law of nature, which is beyond the knowledge both of the ungodly and of weak believers, God never acts, any more than He acts against Himself.[3]

And this is just what I mean: God does not act contrary to himself. If God does a miracle by *intervention*, then we already have both God and the universe in which God intervenes. But if the universe already exists, it already contains that which cannot be violated: the divinely established and universal order, or "the supreme law of nature." Thus, like a divine decree, there is nothing more for miraculous intervention to *do*. All that would be accomplished by it is already accounted for, simply in the creation itself.

Jesus taught us to look upon God as the universe's loving Creator and Father, who notices even the fall of the sparrow. Therefore we believe that the whole thing has sprung from his all glorious, triumphant, infinitely creative and omnipotent heart. Whatever is, in whatever manner it is, exists only insofar as our God has first given it its *is*. All things are, simply through the divine *yes*. Doubtless the creation is infused with potencies which respond better when they align themselves with his will. Still, even these very potencies receive their *could-be* from his hand. Thus, God is only resisted insofar as he has created such a thing to be able to resist him in the first place. Yet God has not decided, nor could he have since he cannot deny himself, to be able to be resisted forever. No *could-be* from God could be *ultimately* evil. If God can be thwarted for a time, even this thwarting is only made to serve his glory—therefore the creature's glory, therefore the universe's glory. Because of the divine creative choice—because what is made comes from an all-loving and powerful Maker—the evil which may infect

3. http://www.newadvent.org/fathers/140626.htm.

the universe must necessarily be finite and limited. It must finally, of necessity, serve the good. Since we have this God—the Christian God, the God of Jesus, who comes to us with a Father's face—the freedom to do evil can never result in infinite harm or corruption. Even the evil of an individual choosing thing must be woven into the divine harmony of life everlasting. Otherwise evil would be as strong in its direction as good is. Evil would be as powerful as good—as good as good—for it, like good, would be power itself. But this cannot be. Evil cannot be both the living fruit and the rottenness which plagues it. Sin and its effects cannot be equally counterbalanced with righteousness and its effects. Therefore whatever comes of sin cannot be eternal and infinite. Such must be bent to the glory and beauty of God.

What then does it matter if there were an historical Adam? What central doctrine of the omnipotent and perfect loveliness of God do we lose in either case? What problem of the human condition is solved; what light now shines to help us walk on our way; what new faith now gives us hope? Or do you think we need more than the doctrine of God's perfect Fatherhood? It cannot be, else we would draw life otherwise than from life itself. Set against the belief in God's invincible and all-tender love, belief in the origin of our first parents is a triviality, a curious speculation. It solves nothing and removes no difficulty. I do not say that the realities of the transgression of Adam, his historical existence, or original sin are meaningless. I only say that they should always be framed in the larger reality of the All-Beautiful who made them.

All difficulties regarding the origin of our race are feints. They are all pushed back, and therefore ultimately resolved in, our God. What is the purpose and character and loveliness of God? What is the human response to the mystery of him? Were our hearts to rest content in a God of all-relation, of perfect love, of sweetest salvation, we could be descended from Satan himself, and all would be well. For at the root of all would be the deeper connection between us as children to God as Father, and that is all we need.

It is to this Father—this primal All-Relating—that our Lord appealed when he said, on behalf of his brothers and sisters, "Forgive them, for they know not what they do."

7

For They Know Not

"And Jesus said, "Father, forgive them;
for they know not what they are doing."
Luke 23:34

Christ says in the Gospel of Luke: "Father forgive them, for they know not what they do." It matters nothing to my purpose if these words exist in the original manuscript. For the principles that they convey—of loving one's enemy, of forgiving those who wrong you, of the impossibility of an *absolutely* evil action, and one, therefore, *deserving* of eternal death—these principles, I say, are found elsewhere, not only in the New Testament, but in all teaching since Plato. Did Christ not also teach us to pray for those who persecute us? And did not the author of John, in his prologue, say that the very same souls who come into the world by the light that lighteth everyone, do not themselves *know* that light and that, because of *ignorance*, they did not accept it? Such things have been known since the race knew enough to be able to write down its own thoughts. Thus I say it matters not whether in the passage of St. Luke we have the very words the Lord spoke as he was making his way to the cross. It is enough for me that, if the words *were* inserted, they were inserted by one who knew and felt the heart of Jesus, and wanted that heart to be present in the text.

Indeed, does not the very insertion of the words—*if* they were inserted—pay homage to their undeniably grand ideal? Or do you think that Christ did not even once think, towards those who were persecuting him and crucifying him, "Father, forgive them"? If you say he did not, I say he could not have perfectly identified with humanity. He could not have been the one who bore all our sins in himself, including the sin of ignorance and hate. The soul of Christ expanded to heights infinite, thus his capacity for compassion was infinite. You cannot imagine an act of compassion that falls outside the sphere of the compassion of Jesus. However high you go, however great you expand, Jesus Christ shall be there, towering over all. I do not say he looked lightly on sin and hate. Yet he must—since he knew their character and since he entered into all human pain and fear—have felt for the souls who were interpenetrated with sin and evil. And if this was the mind of Christ, and if he truly saw human souls this way, what matters about some words in a text, which he may or may not have said with his mouth, then and there? We want to know Jesus' *heart*. If that heart was indeed infinitely human and infinitely compassionate and forgiving, then such words dwelt there, even if they did not go forth from his lips at the recorded moment.

The will follows the intellect. What the intellect proposes to the will, the will assents to, since the nature of the will is just to assent to that which appears to it good. If the intellect ever presented to the will some irresistible good—some good which had no defect, some good which was absolutely and in all respects good—the will would assent to such with absolute fearlessness and joy. Many imagine the next life in light of this fact, and it stirs in them a hope unspeakable. *Up there*, as Dante would say, the intellect sees God face to face, and God, being unveiled in his infinite goodness and beauty, presents to the will that which it sees clearly and which it cannot but cling to and enjoy in expansive satisfaction. Would not such loveliness come in waves ever-new and forms innumerable to the finite consciousness, without shadow of want or need unmet, for all eternity? The soul, having within it a never-ending well-spring of the divine life, would, if it sighed at all, sigh for pleasure's sake, or in anticipation of some new glory that should visit it, in God's sweet time.

Yet there are some Christians who hold that there is an act of will regarding some object which, once committed, could possibly foil this destination, this glorified enjoyment of God. There are certain things one may do, they say, that, if done, *merit* eternal torment and separation from our Maker. Such acts have been called "mortal sins." Against this teaching I ask, when such a sin occurs, does the soul know for certain that the good it apprehends as desirable will, if chosen, *in fact*, cause to itself this irreparable, unspeakable torment? And if it does, and if the will chooses the thing anyway, I ask: is not the will then already corrupted before its choice, in its very desiring of the bad thing? Is the nature of the will such that the intellect could show it something altogether horrible for it, yea, the worst thing imaginable—eternal torment, eternal godlessness—and the will be even *able* to desire this? If yes, how could such a faculty even be a will, since the will is just that which has appetite towards the good *as understood*? If such a thing—such a power of desiring and choosing—existed, it is plain to say that no one would want it. For who would want a power that could desire that which the intellect saw as the worst evil thinkable, an evil which, if chosen, would lead to the worst consequence imaginable?

On the other hand, if the intellect does not know for certain that the desired thing leads to such a fate—and thinks therefore that the thing in question is not an *absolutely* wicked thing to choose—how is it true that the will fully *consents* to choose the object which *actually* leads to its own absolute wickedness and eternal death? If the soul is not fully and unmistakably aware that choosing the desired object will certainly bring about eternal torture or destruction to itself, why then does the soul *deserve* those consequences, seeing as it does not consent with a responsible knowledge of all that its choosing entails?

"But, if we knew for *certain* that certain acts led us to eternal life as a reward, people would do the acts not because the acts were good in themselves, but only to get the reward. Thus we would have an end of virtue."

To this I ask: are you asserting that, in fact, you as a Christian *do not* know for certain which acts lead to an eternal reward? If so, how then can you say that there *are* certain acts that keep us from such? Are we certain only of the mere existence of the acts, but ignorant of what they are? What! Are we certain that there is poison in *one* of the drinks of life, but unable to know which? Can we not know the only thing we absolutely must know in order to have life and hope in God?

If we are so ignorant—if certainty is in principle impossible because it would destroy virtue—why continue to erect a system explaining what one must do to avoid damnation? If we do not know what leads to heaven, then surely we do not know what leads to hell, seeing as one way of getting to heaven is avoiding hell. If "avoiding mortal sin" is a logically necessary condition for attaining salvation, then we either know for certain how to avoid mortal sin and therefore know for certain how to obtain the reward we are after, or we do not. If we do not, then we may as well be silent about heaven and hell, seeing as we have as much knowledge of how to reach them as we do of reaching an unreachable. Yet if we say we do have certain knowledge, then the objection fails, and we arrive back at explaining how it is conceivable for someone to knowingly choose that which will bring upon him unspeakable and irremediable ruin.

What it comes to is this. In sinning, either the person does not, in fact, know that such a choice will bring upon them unimaginable eternal torment and they act in ignorance, or they know such a thing and act from an appetite already defective.

All people necessarily desire happiness. A person cannot will to be unhappy, for "willing" just is to desire, and to desire just is to wish for happiness. That this is a truism does not make it false. Indeed, for those whose hearts long to connect to the thinkers of history, it should please them to reflect that this philosophy of human nature runs from Aristotle to Aquinas to Luther to Boyd. It is a manifest contradiction to suppose that a will would want anything other than something that appears pleasant to it, for "want" just is the appetite for something that appears pleasant. Thus the actual existence of a sin that is truly mortal—a sin in which the evil act was apprehended in all its seriousness as something which necessarily entailed a pain that infinitely outweighed any pleasure—is impossible. Insofar as the mind cannot but judge a thing as true which appears to it true, in that same degree, if it truly apprehends an action as bringing about irremediable ruin, the will cannot possibly desire that such an act be committed. How then are the conditions necessary for a mortal sin in principle even possible? If full knowledge is present, deliberate consent cannot be; if deliberate consent is present, full knowledge cannot be.

A wicked act, therefore, insofar as it leads to a separation from God who is very Goodness itself, is just that far away from a true and full and real act of will. It is an act of will not yet faithfully enlightened by an intellect that fully beholds the truth.

There is a second difficulty attending the idea of mortal sin, which is the impossibility of *defining* one. If we were really capable of committing a mortal sin, surely, if we were to be responsible for avoiding one, we ought to know without doubt what exactly one was. Or if there were many such sins, we ought to know exactly what each of them were. How else purposefully avoid them? But since a necessary factor in determining whether a sin is mortal in the first place is knowing the state of one's intention, and since no one can know his own intention perfectly (let alone the intention of his neighbor), then no one can really know whether he has committed any such sins. He cannot even know, upon considering his next act, if such an act, in the final analysis of God's clear and perfect light of judgment, will be mortally grievous! Nor would a clear conscience necessarily amount to an objectively innocent one, for is not "the heart devious above all else"[1]? A misplaced word here, a duty left undone there, could lead to eternal torment! Who knows? If only one more ounce of strength had been given—the exact amount being impossible to know beforehand, it being known with certainty only to God—an act may have been, although not praiseworthy, at least not mortal! If the sinner had but submitted his intellect to what he never could have been sure of, he *then* would have been saved from the fatal error!

Although it is out of the abundance of the heart that words flow forth from the lips and thoughts spring into the mind, when we attempt to judge the outer layers of the self which we see in our actions, by the inner layers of the self which hide within the caverns of our consciousness, who can be confident about what he sees? Who can map out the labyrinthine mazes of the heart, the recesses of the subconscious? Who can put his finger on the ever-elusive *me*, to be sure of it? Yet if one cannot know his own intentions, and if he cannot then trust in God to surely and necessarily correct him when his intentions are not what they ought to be, then no one can have anything more than a guess as to whether they've committed, are committing, or are in danger of committing such sins!

Do you say that although one cannot *know* his intentions are pure, nevertheless, he can have *signs* that they are? What, I ask, are these signs? Pleasure at reading the Bible, or going to church, or thinking about Jesus? But these things are found even in wicked people, indeed sometimes they are most present in the most wicked. It is not a hard thing to deceive oneself and therefore justify oneself and rest content in oneself concerning the Bible, or church, or Christ. But more than this, the matter of *interpreting* a sign of the heart's purity carries with it the same difficulty as interpreting one's own intentions. How could you not know your intentions, but know the *signs* of your intentions? A sign is simply the outward showing of an inner reality. When the reality bubbles up and bursts out of the self, it thereby

---

1. Jer 17:9

produces the sign. To know whether a sign is present, then, one must know what is already causing it to come to be. To the sign in question which we are interpreting therefore we must ask: it is produced by an *appropriate* pleasure in the things of God, or an *inappropriate*? Does the sign reveal an *ordinate* will, or an *inordinate*? Yet to even possibly answer such questions requires possessing the very thing that is said to be impossible to begin with: knowledge of one's intentions towards God!

It is for this reason that our God must be kind enough towards us to never require our relationship to him to be one of bondage to the letter. A system which requires certainty of our intentions in order to have peace of mind and true love towards God is a system only Satan could devise. How could you trust that God loved you—how could you ever have peace towards him—if God created your necessarily uncertain nature—indeed created you such that certainty was a thing impossible to you—and yet demanded certainty from you, on pain of eternal agony?

To be *able* to be out of the good graces of God—what is this but to say that it is *possible* for God to stop loving you? Some say that we can hope in God's salvation, but we cannot *presume* that we shall attain it. To which I ask, can we presume that God loves us and is working towards our happiness? How have hope without presumption? How believe without assenting with the mind that the thing is *so*? Would you tell me that hope can exist without faith? Or either without love? Verily, no. If we believe that God loves us, yea, and is Love itself, surely it is no bad thing to believe that he cannot even possibly hate us. Do you think very Love would be *offended* at the boldness of the thought, friend: that God cannot do anything less than love you infinitely? To think that Love is troubled, nay angered, by our presuming on its action! The absurdity of the idea makes the child-heart in me almost laugh.

We must be able have confidence in what we know—that is, in what we are convicted of in our conscience regarding our own heart's intentions. If we cannot even have this, we can trust neither God nor ourselves, and all talk of having confidence in "external signs" is meaningless.

"Still, if one commits a mortal sin, whether or not he knows it, in reality, charity is extinguished in the heart, and that heart *cannot* love God."

How is it conceivable that there be absolutely no charity—no love at all—in a human heart? You have asserted the strangeness; shall you not explain it? Without desire and love in some form, how could a human being consciously act or think? Such action may no doubt be unconscious;

and that may be your rebuttal. But so too would remain my point. For how could human action, unmoved by love and unconscious, be truly *human* action? How could it be intentional; how could it be reaching *towards*? So long as a human is conscious and has some movement of will, he has the love of something—of *some* good—however feebly the movement of will and judgment may be. Therefore from the very fact that one consciously thinks and wants at all, he necessarily has some degree of love in him, however dim.

"But charity is the love of human for God, whereas mere natural love is the love of the human for something created. The second can exist without the first."

I ask, when we are called to choose between loving God and loving creature, do we truly see the essence of God? If we do, how could one ever choose against him and sin, God being necessarily irresistible, when seen? Yet if we do not see God's essence, or if it is there but we cannot fully see it, how can there be the division which the system itself calls for? To consciously choose one object in place of another, that other must be present to consciousness. If I choose x rather than y, both x and y must be objects of my perception. But those who hold to such a teaching of sin admit that no one sees God as an object of choice or perception. We see him only through created things. In all choices, then, all we perceive are created things. How then can one ever choose a created thing *absolutely* over and against God?

Let me suppose for the sake of argument that such an absurd state of "extinguished charity" could exist in a body housing a live soul made in the image of God. Now, granting this, some say that should one *die* in this state of extinguished charity, it is only *then* that he deserves hell. Now notice first this inconsistency. Is it the *committing* of the sin which deserves hell, or the *dying* in the state of *having committed* the sin? The case is different because, if the former, the person is immediately deserving of hell the moment he commits the sin. If the latter, then the person does not deserve hell until the moment of his death. This is relevant because if one truly deserves hell the moment of committing mortal sin, he *then* becomes objectively guilty, and therefore on this scheme *then* loses all his worth as a child of God created for happiness. If such is true, why ought any Christian pray for those whom they suspect may be in a state of mortal sin? They literally deserve hell, right then, given their current state of extinguished charity. There is nothing in them which is objectively worth saving, worth perfecting in heaven. If there were, they would have some speck of divinity—and, therefore, charity—in them. They would retain their human dignity and value. But of course they cannot have dignity or value, or else they would not *deserve* to be tortured or destroyed for eternity. Does such a teaching not mean that, to pray for the immortal soul of a person in a state of mortal sin—supposing for a moment it were coherent to say a soul could exist without any trace of its Maker, it somehow having the power to extinguish the principle of life in itself and yet still remain a soul at all—does such a teaching, I say, not mean that if it were even possible to conceive of such an un-human being existing without charity, that to pray for its salvation would be essentially unjust? Would it not be wishing for an immoral, unjust thing: the renewing of charity in a soul that deserves eternal separation from God?

Do the saints in heaven pray for the damned? If not, is it not because the damned *deserve* their punishment? What then is the difference in praying for this soul who deserves hell now but has not yet gone there, and praying for that soul who deserves it now and is there already?

"Because the first has not yet died and may be saved. The second has died, and his fate set."

You then admit the inherit punishment that is due to both is the same. You say only that, for some reason, we ought to *prefer* that punishment not occur to one, and instead occur to the other. But if the second equally deserves God's justice, and if it is good to rejoice in this justice, why not desire this justice—which gives joy to the saved in heaven, by the way—to take place in the first? The mere fact that justice has not yet been carried out does nothing to remove the fact that it *ought* to be. The whole difficulty remains. It is not alleviated by appeals to the mere current situation of the creature. Thus I ask again, how would wishing and praying for a soul in mortal sin not be *unjust*? If hell is God's justice, and if we hope that such a justice is not carried out in the sinner, we are hoping that God's justice does not take place in one in whom it ought to take place—one in whom it would be just for it to take place. How therefore are we not hoping and praying for injustice?

"It may not be just to pray for the soul living in mortal sin, but it is loving, and we are commanded to love all people."

To be commanded to love all people! As if that was not the natural, the only true way of things! Can one be loving but not just to his fellow human, or just and not loving? If so, how shall one choose which to be? Is either one better than the other? If so, why? And why then ever is the opposite?

Let me return to my point. I ask, what, precisely, is a mortal sin?

Ears of Corn

One answers, "A mortal sin is the placing of one's last end in a creature."

I ask, what does that mean, *precisely*? You say we cannot know God himself. All we know are his created effects. To which I ask, if all we know of God are his created effects, how is it possible to know if one is truly loving God, or merely his effect? On the system here erected, whereby God sits outside of and beyond the experience of his creation, and where he commands obedience on pain of eternal torture, there must be an utter division between the two. Since it is possible to sin in such a way to place the creature above a God which can never be seen or known, both God and the creature competitively fight for worship. If we cannot know God himself, how choose him without choosing one of his creatures, the only things which we *can* know? Am I able to love God only through the creature, and yet threatened with damnation for loving him by loving his creation?

On such a scheme of possible mortal sin, how can one know whether the enjoyment of a particular "created effect"—the effect itself not being God himself and therefore able to be loved more than him—how can one know if his enjoyment is loving God's effect in the right way, or with the right proportion? Could not the slightest enjoyment of some creaturely pleasure—the laughter of a friend, the smiling eyes of a cat, the kiss of a lover, the taste of a fruit—be inordinately directed towards the creature and away from God? Note well how crucial the question is. For if the proportion of our love of God and creature is wrong, we shall suffer never-ending pain. Nor can we have peace in our uncertainty, for you have said that we can have no hope in an all-loving God who *necessarily* sets us right. Such trust, you have told us, may be a forbidden *presumption*.

The problem is not that there are no *lists* of mortal sins (there are many, in catechisms abundant). The problem is that such lists do not capture the essence of mortal sin itself, which is the *inordinate* love of creature. Just what *is* this inordinate love of creature? We must know, must we not? May the only thing that can damn us be that which it is impossible for us to discover? Or do you take the question less seriously than your theology truly demands? Do you really believe that which you claim to be a revelation, if you are not infinitely concerned with the question?

I ask again. How can one know if his love of a creature—that is, his passion, his desire, his concern for it—how can one know if such is too great? You cannot say he may know it through God's very teaching him by life experience that such is wrong. For God may not do that, and may give him over—justly—to eternal torment or destruction after a single commission of the thing in question. The answer therefore must be known beforehand. Must not law must be understood, so that it will not be broken? Otherwise what help is there for the soul who stands in potency to sin? Before it acts, it would be true to its God and be saved from damnation; therefore it must know: what is and is not an act of *inordinate* love?

We would be saved, learned teacher of systems! Therefore, tell us: what *is* a mortal sin? Is a doctrine which rests on a theory in principle impossible to define, itself capable of being believed, of being comprehended, of being loved?

Observe clearly the practical implications of the idea that a human could even possibly perform some act which, once done, meant that justice required that it experience eternal conscious torment. It follows on such a teaching that, since no one can know his intentions certainly, and since to avoid such a sin, it is necessary that one not intend to place his last end in a creature rather than God, no person can ever know if any act he deliberates about will be mortally sinful. This is simply the logical conclusion of the doctrine. If, when one acts, one cannot know his intentions, and if one's intentions must not be inordinately directed towards a creature, then no one can know which of his actions, no matter how small, could possibly result in his own eternal torment. Even if one were to remove himself from all his fellow creatures, he could always inordinately love the creature of himself. In looking at himself as an object, he could never be sure of his own valuation of that self's intentions, toward both himself and his God. Any choice therefore could be mortally sinful. If this sounds unbelievable, it is not from any fault in the argument. It is simply from an emotional attachment to and innate trust in the goodness and love of God, which makes such a state of human existence seem impossible for him to create, because too hellishly angst-ridden.

If a doctrine of mortal sin were true, I ask, how could one ever truly make a decision? Would not the sheer paralysis of choosing that which may result in eternal misery overwhelm the mind? The fact that people often deliberate and often do that which they think sinful is not to the point, for it only proves that people do not really believe in the possibility of mortal sins at the time of their acting. But again I am not attacking what people believe when they make choices. I am attacking a theory of the divine-human relation which says that a loving God, who not only expects but wills that we trust and love him, could create us even capable of committing such a thing. If God loves us—and if he does not, trying to understand

and therefore obey him is meaningless—how can our relation to him be accurately described by a doctrine which makes mortal sin possible?

To see the point more clearly, take a normal example often seen in stories. Suppose you had to diffuse a bomb by cutting the right wire out of two. Suppose also that, should the bomb blow, it would cause, not instant death, but protracted, unimaginable torture for all eternity. Were the wrong wire cut, you would be eternally separated from all that you loved, and you would be in mental anguish without any relief, forever. Further, you would *know* that this state would never end, with utmost certainty. You could not even begin to believe that your suffering would be lessened even the slightest, since such a feeling would amount to hope, and hope, being a gift of God, would find no place in you. Now imagine that this is what happens if you cut one of the wires. On the other hand, if you cut the other wire, you would continue to exist in your current state.

Now, say you knew all this with utmost certainty. Say that these ideas were the liveliest realities before your mind: you absolutely *knew* them to be true and *believed* them. And now, finally, say that you absolutely *had* to cut one of the wires.

Who could even make such a choice? The more one believed the reality of what he held to be true, the more impossible would he find it to choose. And insofar as one did choose, all that would prove was that at that moment he simply did not believe that the imagined outcome was really possible. Of course it would be no wonder if this occurred. No rational person could actually *make* such a choice unless he engaged in self-deception. Unless, that is, he ceased believing in the reality of the possibility of eternal torture, which is the whole point.

I say that if the mind truly were convinced of the scenario set before us—with the wire representing a committed mortal sin that puts one helplessly out of the grace of God, where he shall necessarily remain unless God freely does for him that which he cannot in any way do for himself—if, I say, such a relation was really believed to exist between humanity and God, paralysis would consume the human mind. It would be simply overwhelmed with the possibility of what may befall it, and could not even think, let alone live, or laugh, or love.

I trust it was this nauseating and unavoidable uncertainty about one's own intentions, and about being unsure just *what* mortal sins were or if he had committed any, that drove Luther to his madness—and therefore his faith. Such ambiguity, such *unknowability*, was the dilemma that spring-boarded him to his *sola fide*. If one cannot not know what mortal sins are or what one's own intentions are when he acts, he can at least know that he has faith: for faith just is the awareness of one's intentional state of belief. To say—or even to *want* to say—"I believe" is to believe already.

As I touched on above, this problem of uncertainty is compounded by the fact that, on certain doctrines of mortal sin, the dilemma of cutting the wire is one which could, theoretically, attend literally every moral decision. Since every decision could also theoretically be a moral one—for cannot any created good be misused if it is loved inordinately?—and since humanity is the type of creature capable, according to St. Paul, of directing *everything* it does to God, then any deliberate action could conceivably be mortally sinful. When I sit down to enjoy my food, do I momentarily forget God, and so cling unworthily to his creation? After all, I do not always thank him, but often plunge myself into the thing forgetfully. When I bow my head to say my prayers, is my mind unduly distracted, not being absolutely absorbed in the Most High God, who I cannot but contemplate without using images of his creation, who nevertheless demands my singular and wearilous attention? When I attend the words of a book, and when my soul is moved by the emotion which they rouse, am I turning from my God to a work of man?

I ask, when I look into my spouse's eyes and feel in my heart that I would gladly die for her, do I love her more than I ought? What if God told me to cease loving her? He could do this on your system, could he not? Yet I have thought that I could not be truly happy unless I knew that she would one day be truly happy too, unless I knew that she too was necessarily precious to God. How could I be a loving child of God if my lover was not one also? Do I not, after all, *love* her? I have often thought, sometimes against my will, that God could not be God unless he loved her and all humanity as much as he could. Is this me putting my will above the will of God, which may or may not will her salvation, which may or may not tolerate her own eternal destruction, which may or may not sit indifferently on his throne as millions of creatures moan in blackest loss and agony forever?

Am I then worthy of damnation for loving that which God commands I not love, but which he has created me loving? Can I love too much, that which was made in his image? Do I justly deserve hell for giving my heart to what he could have just as contingently willed that I withhold it from?

I ask—nay, I cry out—must I have a God who cannot be my God unless I sacrifice all my earthly loves upon his altar? Must there always be a

Ears of Corn

competition between my love of God and my love of his creatures, such that I must always be willing to part with them forever, to become such as if I never knew, never loved them? Lord, I shall gladly give you all that is mine! But how have loving gladness unless I trust that thou art altogether the best for the very loves that I surrender to thee?

It is only one who has not tried to love God with his whole heart, and who has not tried to filter absolutely all his affections and creaturely loves through his Maker, who could find the things I have been describing difficult to imagine. Shame on you, then, if you believe my hypotheticals facetious or unbelievable. I am taking the possibilities of idolatry, along with the justly imposed eternal punishment for such—teachings which I learned from your books and your doctrines—as seriously as humanly possible: as seriously, I say, as all should take them who believe them true. Surely one cannot take a teaching on *eternal* punishment *too* seriously? Surely one cannot try *too* hard to know and do the will of God?

And what of the sickening, too frequently observed fact, that some Christians *joke* about damnation? If some souls really are tormented for eternity, how could a believer make light of this? A man may joke about hell who disbelieves it. I have nothing to say to him. But how could anyone who believed it speak about it from the *pulpit* with flippancy? How could a deep and noble soul, a lover of the human race who nevertheless believes that some shall be lost, how could such a one excite *laughter,* in any form, about hell? Would you laugh if you saw a man butchered, saw a woman die in childbirth, saw a man being boiled alive? But you shall laugh when you hear a reference to a teaching you claim to be as certain as the gospel itself: a soul being tortured, without respite, forever! Are such jests and chuckles not the most heinous shame against your humanity? What could one do to recede further from the love of Jesus than to hear the word hell, think it real, and *smile*? I say, to hold to a belief in endless hell and to make any *joke*, however trivial, is to either cease believing in the reality altogether, or to cease being human—and so deserve it.

Yet I think—at least I hope—that such untroubled moods surrounding the doctrine of hell do much to disprove it by revealing an almost universal trust and comfort in the goodness of God.

I ask again, for I must know—else I could be punished by a God who could hate the creature he created or be foiled at finishing what he set his omnipotence to accomplish—how can I love a created thing too much?

"By breaking one of God's commands in relation to the thing."

To which I ask, are God's commands that alone which gives goodness and rightness to an act? Could God command we do a thing—could he command that which he has not now commanded, or not command that which he has—and the mere commanding make the thing good? If so, then it would be not the act itself but the fact that God has commanded that we not do it which would be wrong. Where then would be the badness in the act? Would it not be indifferent to goodness or badness, and only become so on the supposition that God commanded or prohibited it? You say God can permit what he wills; thus he can permit the very thing that he has, on a supposition, forbidden! Where then is the good in the thing itself? Morality lies in sheer blind obedience to an infinitely arbitrary rule generator!

How trust a God whose morality is what it is on a whim, without law? Could not such a God command that truth tellers be damned; that lovers of justice be sent to torment? Could God command that one damn himself? Could he command that one torture his lover for all eternity? Is there absolutely nothing that God cannot command and it therefore be right? "A thing is right if God says it is." How far can we take such a teaching? Evidently infinitely far, extending to any action conceivable. For if we were to imagine some action which not even *God* could command, because the doing of the thing would be too wicked or terrible, then there is some ultimate limit which not even God's commands can affect. But then we are really admitting that things are good for more than the mere *arbitrary* command of a God that could will otherwise. We are admitting that actions are good because they are, like that will of God himself, *necessarily* good.

Yet if God's mere commands are not that alone which make an act good—if, that is, an act is good because it is necessarily good and cannot but be good in the same way that very wisdom and love themselves cannot be otherwise—then simply appealing to a list of things not to be done *because God said so* does nothing to help us discover what could constitute a mortal sin.

"Yet there are many things which the Bible commands us to do, or forbids us from doing, which cannot be right, for the Bible says that they cannot be done with impunity."

If you think a thing is right and good simply because the Bible says so, then the goodness of the thing lies not in the thing itself, but simply in the Bible's saying that the thing is good. Had the Bible said otherwise, the thing in question would not be good, and so you would believe differently. But if the Bible itself could say absolutely anything—if, that is, there is nothing necessarily good to which the Bible itself conforms its words—then nothing is absolutely good, and morality is nothing other than whatever the words on the page happen to say. Hate and envy, lust and vice, may just as well have been commanded as forbidden. There cannot be anything *intrinsically* wicked about them, else they would stand on their own feet, without additional support from the Bible.

If God did not love us necessarily, then he could possibly hate us. Such a relation between us and he would be a true possibility. Therefore to trust God, we cannot believe it even *possible* for him to be less than our essential helper, deliverer, lover. We *must* think of him as our Father, and us as his children. I say that we must believe, on pain of insanity, or on pain of believing in a God impossible to trust and love, that God is so good that, if he brings us into being, he cannot but necessarily will our perfect loveliness—and therefore the setting of us right. If we did not believe this about him, how could we ever obey him, or trust him, or love him, out of a pure heart? No doubt we would try our very hardest to keep all his rules. Yet never out of love, never out of seeing naturally the necessary loveliness of what he told us to do. We would act purely out of fear of punishment.

"Luckily, I do not believe in a doctrine of mortal sin and keeping a list of *rules*. It is faith alone that saves from hell. Therefore all that you say about our necessary relation to God and our necessary trust in his resolve to set us right touches nothing that I hold."

Though one may say he does not believe in the doctrine of mortal sin, I say, so long as he believes that there is some state of the human condition which *justly deserves* eternal separation from God or eternal conscious suffering, he implicitly believes in a doctrine of mortal sin, though he may repudiate the phrase. For if a person can do anything to get into a state which *merits* for him eternal hell—whether this means being born into a sinful race, or simply possessing or not possessing some state of mental assent—then that state is functionally equivalent to a mortal sin. Doubtless, what falls into the category of "damnable actions" may be different—to one it may be lack of faith; to another, sinning against the Holy Spirit; to another, being a heretic; or any number of things. The point is the same: the category of an eternally damnable action itself exists in the first place. Therefore any who believe in eternal hell also implicitly believe that humanity is capable of doing something to go there. And so all the difficulties I have been speaking of reappear.

Ah, friends, were we strong enough men and women, fear could be present in our consciousness to the highest degree and would serve as no deterrent of our action. Our obedience would be to the necessary goodness that rules existence, not to the consequential evil of pain that attends the fearful motives of our action. To get to this apex of faith, we must purge ourselves of fear, by steeping ourselves in love. St. John tells us: "There is no fear in love, but perfect love casts out fear. For fear has to do with punishment, and he who fears is not perfected in love."[2] We must love the purity of love more than we fear the impurity of fear. Our doubts *must* give way to courageous love, friends. They must! Or we shall go mad. We must never do a thing for God or think a thing about him *simply* because an authority has told us that we must, "or else." The motive behind such action is not devotion or love of truth, nor is it faith, nor love of pureness, nor love of loveliness. It is simply fear. We must love God so fearlessly that we must not be afraid of thinking too highly of him, of trusting him to the uttermost. We must be bold enough to say that when we go wrong, he *will* set us right, for we know not what we do. He wants us to be happy, does he not? This is just what it means for him to love us; and we must trust that he loves us, else believing in him would be useless. And to prove to ourselves that such a wish is no desire for licentiousness, let us commit to return the necessity of his love, with a necessity of our own.

We must therefore trust that even our sins are only possible because we do not yet see God as we shall see him—as he shall have us see him—when sin will be altogether impossible. This is not to say our sins now are anything less than terribly heinous. That which allows a separation, however slight, between creature and Creator, between pure love and love not yet pure, must be the most horribly crucifying reality thinkable. Yet, as terrible as such a state is and the sin that necessarily attends it, it cannot be that we may ever be utterly cut off from the source from which we came. Even were God to annihilate a thing he had made, it would still be true that the thing came from him and from his heart: that it was a divine representation of him. It was something *like* him—therefore, his *child*. How then could he leave it; how could he give up on it?

Since we are altogether from God, the movement of our sin can never be infinite, absolute, or final. An act of sin is not, strictly speaking, the opposite of an act of love. If it were, the badness of sin would equal in its own direction the goodness of love in its direction. But then good and evil would

---

2. 1 John 4:18

be co-equal and co-powerful, which cannot be. The arena and conditions that are necessary for an absolutely evil choice therefore presuppose an impossibility. They presuppose that the mind and will are equally balanced between good and evil, meaning and absurdity, being and non-being. They presuppose that, at the root of all, light is not stronger than darkness, that the tendency of being and life and existence towards the good are not necessary and ultimate, and that, somehow, all such movement and power can be just as strong in the direction of evil. Such a theory imagines that the consequences and effects of evil are infinite by their own essential unreality. If one really could commit a sin which resulted in the utter negation and absolute unmeaning of the purpose for which he was made—this being the essence of hell—then there would be tied in to the very power of choosing evil a consequence and effect as infinite, eternal, and real as what lay in the power of choosing good. But then evil would be as high, as ultimate, as necessarily all-drawing and all-consequential as good itself. Praise God for this: goodness alone is necessity. Such a goodness deemed it "necessary that the Christ should suffer these things and then enter into his glory."

8

Was It Not Necessary?

"Was it not necessary that the Messiah should suffer these things and then enter into his glory?"

LUKE 24:26

THE WORLD IS ALL of a piece. Any part of it, whether thing or space or time or thought, is connected to some other part, and so on, until you have the whole. Posit whatever individual throughout the cosmos—suppose the smallest mite of being existing at any point of space or time or thinking—and, because of the connectedness of the whole, you likewise posit the entire creation. If it were not so, the world would not be one, would not be unifiedly itself, would not be a singular *uni-verse* of God.

To suppose otherwise would be to suppose that the world lacked its own totality. We say that the world is *coherent*. But what does this mean other than that it *co-heres* as a singular? Yet how could this be if *this world* could either be all of what it is—if, that is, it could include a definiteness regarding all its totality of place, time, matter, spirit—or if it could include an indefiniteness regarding these things? What would we mean by calling it *this*? The world itself would have no essential meaning, no identity. It would not be itself. It would be potentially anything and therefore actually nothing.

Ears of Corn

A man generally thinks that things could have been otherwise than they were. He took this way, but he could have taken that way. He married this person, but he could have married that one; he narrowly escaped, but he could have fallen victim to. But supposing the world is itself and supposing it is a unified creation of God and governed by him, this cannot be. When we imagine some part of the world being otherwise, we give reasons why, in fact, it was not. We think, "I took this way, but I could have taken that way," and then think, "but I didn't, *because* of such and such." Thus, we give an explanation for why the world went the way that it did and not otherwise. But this explanation does not show how things could have went otherwise, presupposing the same world and presupposing the same all-connected relation of being in which we exist.

Presuppose some fact in the world that could have been different. Now, if the world is connectedly intelligible, then there must be some reason in the world why the fact was what it was. We went this way because we needed such and such, or married this person because we fell in love, or escaped because we turned aside at the last moment. Since *these* reasons existed, the *event* was what it was rather than otherwise. Take the reasons away and could the event still be posited? We see the reason why the thing occurred. It occurred because of such and such. And such and such itself happened for some reason, and so on. Therefore, the event under discussion was not—could not have been—different, unless you presuppose some *additional* or *different* reason: I needed such and such, *but* I was running late, so did not get it. But here again, we are not showing how a thing could have been different, but only stating why it was what it was in the first place, and why it occurred when it did. How could the event have been different, I ask? By different factors coming to bear on it, you reply. But different factors entail circumstances not identical. Therefore the point is not proven, for, granting different circumstances at different times, you have an entirely new all-connected universe.

Often when we explain events, we simply multiply the reasons why the events were so. Each event has its explanation in some prior event, and so on. But if that is how we explain events, and if this method is acceptable, it cannot be the case that the events that occur could have been otherwise, presupposing the prior events that gave rise to them. For an event to truly be able to be other than it was, it must be possible to presuppose exactly the same data leading up to the event and posit two opposite outcomes as equally likely. We must be able to say, "Given x, therefore, either y or not y."

Now, if this could be, then there would be no reason why a thing happens in the world rather than not, for any reason we give to explain an event could itself have failed to be. We never arrive at a necessity, but push back infinitely into contingency.

In a world where nothing necessarily gave rise to anything else, if we pointed to the reason why an event occurred, that reason would not account for the event, for *even given the reason*, the event could either follow subsequently, or not. Otherwise, granting the reason, the event is necessary. The event's happening or not happening thus is equally possible, given the preceding reason, which we conveniently call a "cause." Why then did the event happen rather than not? If indeterminism is true, in principle, this question can have no answer. The event is inexplicable. Its not happening is as equally reasonable as its happening. Since no reasons necessitate, no reasons explain. Their existence is as equally indeterminate as what they give rise to. Do we suppose we could point to a free agent to explain the event? What about that free agent though? We cannot point to some state of mind, some internal feeling, some movement of will. For all such things, remember, are not reasons which actually explain the event, since, given all the same datum, the event could either follow or not. All we can do is point to the agent as a whole and say, "The event came from the agent, but not for any reason *in* the agent. The agent simply produced the event spontaneously. He could have just as likely—given all the same preceding phenomenon of will, mind, feeling, and intent—not produced it. The event therefore is totally unrelated to the agent, for the cause is unrelated to the effect."

Who could accept such an account of the universe's relation; who could live in the world one moment if he believed it? Would the notion not destroy science, destroy action, destroy our very way of understanding the world and ourselves? If a man could will to move his arm, and if that could lead equally to a state of rising his arm, or not, without presupposing some additional factors which explained why it was raised or not, where is the intelligibility—the knowability—of creation? Or if a man could go from a state of not willing to willing, without some cause necessarily moving him—say a desire now becoming present, or a sound argument now turning his thought—how could man be a comprehensible, a *rational*, being? Practical reason operates under the assumption that effects necessarily follow from their causes. It can make no practical judgment at all unless it assumes this. It *must* suppose "if x, therefore, y." It cannot operate

Ears of Corn

if it supposes "if x, therefore either y or not y." At that moment it becomes merely speculative and stands suspended in paralysis. No doubt we often speculate, and no doubt practical reason is often mistaken. But for action to occur, we must finally settle on some "if x then y" that we suppose for the moment to be necessary.

All this amounts to the connectedness of the world and the necessary relation of its causes and effects. Given a cause under certain conditions, an effect must follow. That is just what a "cause" is: that which gives rise to an effect. Otherwise, the cause is no more a cause nor the effect any more an effect, and the two are unrelated.

I ask, if the world has no necessary nature, why should nature uniformly produce the same effect? Given all the same data fed into nature, if *everything* could be other than it is, then the fact that it continues to behave as predictably as it does is inexplicable. It may just as well behave otherwise. Do you say nature must behave naturally? Then you presuppose a natural and essential relation between cause and effect in the world, in nature herself. That is, you believe nature—at least this nature in this observed world—is self-coherent, necessarily itself, and imbued with logos. She has *laws*. But then her causes are necessarily related to her effects, and there is an essential and necessary unity to the world.

Aristotle's argument against the idea that all things take place by necessity amounts to this: if it were so, deliberation would be in vain. But this does not follow. For if all that occurs in the world occurs necessarily, then deliberation *cannot* be in vain, for it infallibly produces its effect. Indeed *nothing* in the world could even *possibly* be in vain, for all things are necessarily and inextricably connected to what they produce.

In fact, Aristotle's reasoning here refutes itself. If causes really are indeterminate towards their effects, it is only *then* that deliberation could *ever* be in vain. For, supposing a person deliberates, a different choice than the one he intended could still come about if effects don't necessarily follow their causes. Indeed what difference would deliberation as such make, if we could suppose the exact kind of deliberation all the way up to the moment of the decision, and if an opposite decision could equally come about?

In no way does the necessity of which I speak deny freedom. A person is free to assent to truth when it appears to him true, and to pursue goodness when it appears to him good. He is free to be himself, free to be what he will be, free to exercise his own will and walk in the air of his own being. Yet his freedom is denied this much: he is not free to be an unintelligibility.

Was It Not Necessary?

No one is free to think that a thing is true that his mind infallibly delivers to him as untrue, nor to pursue goodness in any other form than what appears to him as good. If necessity denies freedom, it denies it in the only possible way that freedom can be denied: by saying it is not free to be unfree. True, humanity is not free to negate itself, negate its desire for goodness nor its understanding of first principles. But does this mean that humanity is unfree? Verily, no. And thank God!

The arguments against the necessity of the connectedness of the world and the necessary relation of the world's causes to its effects stem from the imaginative and unfounded idea that, if it were true, all our choices would be meaningless. But this cannot be. For in a world that a good God has made, nothing can be meaningless, nothing useless, nothing vain. Each thing is situated so as to produce the flowering effect that it is divinely destined to bring about, yea, even to the perfecting of every individual creature that God has made. Once each creature has filled up for itself the measure of learning and the taste of existence that God has made necessary for its completion, it enters into its joy, being thus brought into its new mode of life. This is the predestination of God: to direct all souls to the glory that they are necessarily fitted for.

"Do you not then contradict the apostle? Does Paul not say, or rather does his logic not demonstrate, that God has predestined only *some* for glory?"

If Paul did say such a thing, or if his logic implied that God predestined some conscious souls to hell, then he lied and spoke an absurdity. He preached the utter and absolute nihilism of creation. For if, granting that human beings exist, and granting that they have the desire for heavenly bliss, and granting also that it makes no difference to God whether they attain it—since God could create them either to attain it or not, indifferently—then their actual attaining it must also be indifferent. But then the glorification of the creature is as insignificant to the world as the glorification of an abstract number. We should then no more rejoice over a person's salvation than lament his damnation. Like one's view of the inspiration of Scripture, if one's theory of apostolic authority, or if the logical deductions of an apostle's words, leads to nihilism, so much for one's theory and deductions. For if nihilism is true, neither theory nor deduction is valuable enough to mean anything, let alone give us eternal life.

But I am not convinced that the apostle *did* teach that God predestined only some for heaven and left others for eternal torture, nor that such a relation between God and creature ever entered into his mind.

You say that God predestines the elect and others he passes by. The elect cannot be lost—they are eternally secure—and the reprobate cannot be saved. Do you affirm this?

"Yes, Christ cannot lose any of his sheep, and the saints will most certainly persevere."

Is it then possible for the elect now living to be lost?

"We do not claim to know who is or is not elect."

I do not ask about the certainty of *whether* one is elect, but the certainty of whether, *if he is elect*, his damnation is possible. No doubt you grant that there is a fact of the matter whether one is elect or not. So I ask again: supposing one is elect, is it possible for him to be lost?

"No."

What then did Christ save the elect one from?

"Damnation."

Yet you just said that the elect could never have been damned, even possibly, since from all eternity God had predestined them. If you say that God elects some who cannot be lost, and who are therefore infallibly saved, then those he elects were never truly able to be damned in the first place. How then criticize the notion of universal salvation by saying it robs humanity of their being saved from their sins? If the elect could not have been lost but can enjoy their heaven, why cannot all mankind enjoy their heaven, even though they were never destined to be lost?

Furthermore, how claim that our actions, which necessarily produce God's ordained effects, are irrelevant, if all are saved? You say if all are necessarily saved, our actions are meaningless. Yet if the elect are necessarily saved, how are their actions meaningful? You say that to pray for salvation is absurd, if God saves all. How is your prayer for your own elect soul not absurd, if you are one of the elect?

"But I do not know who is predestined or not or whether I am elect. Therefore I pray that I may be sure that I am."

Even on your own theory, your ignorance does nothing to change the ontological fact that, right now, you are either elect, or not. There is truth or falsity to the statement: "John Doe is elect." Thus your destiny is fixed by God's decree and impossible to be otherwise. An appeal to ignorance does nothing to remove the difficulty.

"Is this not a dangerous doctrine? Our efforts for salvation, for example, make little sense if it is impossible to be lost."

That does not follow. The false assumption is this: if necessitarianism is true, no matter what I do, z will occur. That is, either x or y—effort or no effort—still z. But this just assumes indeterminism. It assumes that either x or y are both possible, when really, only one is, which is the one that occurs in fact. We call both possible because we do not know which occurs. The objection therefore begs the question. The answer to the question of "Why make an effort to be saved—why pray at all—if all are saved infallibly?" is simply this: because prayer necessarily and infallibly produces its effect. The real mystery would be: why pray for perfection—why try to be saved—if causes do not necessarily and infallibly produce their effects? If indeterminism is true, a cause may either produce its effect or not. Why therefore pray for it?

"The doctrine of limited predestination shows how all our goods are purely gracious gifts from God, and in no way from ourselves. This leads to the most humble praise and destroys all boasting. We do not despair over whether or not we are elect, but rejoice in seeing how good God is for giving us so many undeserved gifts."

Yes, but notice what you deem gifts are not yet known to you to be finally good things. To the non-elect—which you may be—they serve as so many pangs of loss, remorse, and torture in the next life, the length and intensity of which make your current graces—they may be *common* graces—disappear into oblivion. Do you think your spouse a good gift of God, your peace of mind, your bodily health, your friends? Are you warmed at the thought of creation, of your relationships, of the joy of existing? Yet, if you are non-elect—a fact which you can neither know nor change—all these gifts will turn unto you sources of the greatest, most unspeakable woe. And do not forget, on your view there are certainly very many who *are* non-elect. Many will have felt just as you do now about their joy and love of life. How then confidently call such things gifts from God, if your confidence itself rests on the mere arbitrary decree of one who need not love you and who could indifferently grant you transitory blessings, only to stoke with such things the never-ending fire-pains of your soul?

"Is the gift of heaven then not a *free* gift of God? Does he then *have* to give it? If so, where is his graciousness?"

Why must a gift be able to be withheld to be good and true? Between lovers, is not giving a blessed *necessity*? What of the man Jesus and his God?

Ears of Corn

Does the Father *contingently* give himself to the Son, or the Son *contingently* love his Father? How is God's graciousness praised, when he could indifferently damn every soul that we shall ever meet? How can we be truly and lovingly grateful to God for a graciousness which entails the absolute nihilism of humanity? No individual human is himself really worth saving, if God could pass each by. How then rejoice in the salvation of that which never *objectively* should have been saved? Why lament the loss of that which was never worth enough to *justly* move our hearts?

I say then that whatever St. Paul's view of the sovereign predestining of God was, it could not mean that God has elected some to glory and passed others by, consigning them to an endless hell. Although it is not difficult to see why some have found the apostle's words to mean the opposite, we must always remember that not even Paul can contradict the laws of being, which are the laws of love. For the two are the same—the law of God.

We are so concerned with what others think or say! We say to ourselves: "We must find out how *Paul* or *Augustine* or *Aquinas* or *Craig* viewed things. *Then* we will know what to believe." What is this but to say that *we* don't have any faith in God *ourselves*? What is this but to take out our own heart and brain and put in their place those of another? What is the meaning of a lack of faith, if not this? Is this unbelief not what Christ bewailed as he walked the streets of Jerusalem; did it not lay heavy on his heart; did it not arouse his anger?

It is the essence of blind and therefore heartless obedience to hold that, no matter *what* is said, if only it is only said by *so and so*, one would believe it. That whole posture to life and faith is useless, for it is no life or faith at all. How does one have faith if one simply automatically believes what he supposes that another person thinks? And to make matters worse, the one who believes thus blindly does not certainly, or even clearly, *know* what the person thought to whose opinion he clings. What! Has he questioned Paul, has he questioned John, has he questioned Christ himself? Have these men synthezied to him their clashing assertions; have they explained how far conclusions were to be drawn from their words? If not, how then is it reasonable to trust a stretched interpretation, deduced from dead images and words, an interpretation which makes humanity's God into the grossest monster imaginable? If an *interpretation* of God raises deeper issues about the very *nature* of God, how can we hold the interpretation, if in doing so we destroy the nature? If such is faith—to blindly hold that which may annihilate our belief in the All-Beautiful altogether—its entire act, its whole *substance*, devours itself.

If humans are predestined by God to hell, or if God can create a human and not predestine it to its own perfection, then to be created by God could be the worst thing possible to befall a soul. Yet how could this be, when, in truth, to be created by God cannot but be the grandest, most sublime thing imaginable, surpassing the thought of seraphim and cherubim? If God is all glorious—and if he is not, what point is there in hoping in him?—then to be created by him *must* be an unspeakable joy. It cannot *but* be a blessing, a *living* which we shall deliciously unwrap, as the ages expand to infinity. Yet some give us a doctrine which makes us afraid to be predestined by God! They make us fear God's predestination like we do his judgment. But is not the point the same? Is not being judged by an all-lovely being the best thing that could happen to someone in the wrong—that is, to a sinner, to one who has evil in him, and who is not yet fully comfortable in his Father's house? To receive the punishment or judgment which such a God would give, how could it not be but to receive the greatest possible gift? If God is all good, all judgment, like all predestining, must be altogether *for* the one being judged. What? Does the accused suffer? Does it know itself a low and evil thing? Is it tormented? Is it confused about truth? So much the better, for such things must be ultimately the best for it, since they are imposed by an Almighty Love out of which the judged creature itself sprang into being unsolicited.

For those who believe in the providential governance of God, the realization of the necessary relation and connectedness of the world solves many contradictions, whereas ignorance of it leads to many. If you are a Christian and believe in a providential God I ask: if the world is not necessarily causally connected throughout time, how could God ensure the crucifixion of Christ? How could he predestine the outworking of the world, guide its history, and paint it into the picture of his intention? How could he promise that all things work together for good? How could he bring about the singular state of humanity, in which all of us sinners need a savior? Can the end be secured without the means? Or shall at length God *intervene* to secure what he wills to secure? Or did God make a system that inevitably leads, no matter which free path, to the *final* result he intended? Yet how would this be any different from supposing that causes must give rise to their effects? It is still true that, given that God creates the world in such a way (x), an outcome (y) infallibly occurs. Are we to suppose that God has no *particular* intention in his creation? That his intention is merely for the world's spontaneous development into *either-this-or-that*, but that he has no *singular* goal in mind? Even still, we cannot disconnect God's causality from the necessity of the world's being what it is, for, supposing God intended pure indeterminacy as such, the world would still *necessarily* be indeterminate.

If you are a Christian who believes in miracles I ask: where would the miraculous be without the necessarily *natural* course of events? We say that a human walking on water is miraculous because, *naturally* speaking, humans do not walk on water. We say it is miraculous for a blind man to see because, *naturally*, blind men cannot see. But if the nature of the human is not such as to necessarily be a single nature which gives rise to natural powers and abilities, what would be unnatural, what would be *miraculous*, about a miracle? If causes in the world do not necessarily produce their effects, and if natures are not necessarily determined to be what they are, then there is no longer any way to call a thing miraculous, for one nature could produce any kind of thing spontaneously. For all we know or could say, the miraculous—the *supernatural*—is just as possible, given the presupposed data, as the *natural*.

Or what about God's knowledge? If you are a Christian who believes that God knows the world I ask: could the world be different than what he knows it to be? What I mean is, supposing that God knows the world, must not then the world be as he knows it?

"But we need not suppose God knows the world."

Oh? The world exists; we cannot suppose it does not, for to suppose that the world did not exist, we would first have to exist in the world to suppose so. Therefore, necessarily, if we are to suppose at all, we must suppose that the world in which we are supposing exists. But if the world exists, God must know it. The world does exist; therefore, it must be as he knows it.

"God is his knowing of all truths, even contingent truths. But contingent truths could be otherwise. Therefore, God could know other than he does."

But then, God could be both knowing p and knowing not-p. But then God himself is in a contingent state. Contingent states need to be caused, else they would not be contingent. But what then would cause God's contingency? What higher principle can exist, above the necessary I AM? Where is the common factor in God knowing p and God knowing not-p, that would be the same in God in either case? Is the Infinite Being of God divisible; can he be added to? Is God's knowledge something tacked on to himself, even though he already contains an infinite fullness? Where would his new knowledge find room? What potential exists in him which is not already exhausted by him, simply by him being himself?

If therefore God knows and orders the world, what God knows and orders in the world must necessarily occur as God knows and orders it. Which is to say that the world's becoming—its movement from past to future as well as its relations among itself—is necessarily connected to God's creating the world. And God's creating the world is necessarily connected to God himself. If then God is necessarily God, the world is necessarily the world.

"Does this not deny possibility? If the world cannot be otherwise, what then does the word mean?"

Possibility refers not to a thing's ability to be other than it is when it is, but to its actually being what is it, when it is, or what it will be, when it will be. That is, a thing is possible only if it comes to be. A seed is possibly a tree, only if in fact it becomes one. If there is no time in which this seed becomes a tree, if God never knew such a thing in his eternal knowledge, and if he never willed it in his infinite and necessary will, it is not possible for the seed to be a tree. This is because the world that exists is one: its truths are one, its relations are one; its beings are one. All these things exist eternally in the mind and will of God, who for his own part eternally creates and is related to the world. If such were other than they were, God would know differently and do differently than he does, which cannot be, or God is not the infinite fullness of himself and could himself be otherwise; he could therefore fail to be God.

As it is commonly understood, possibility resides solely in our imagination. When we say *I could have gone this way*, that does not mean that, in the actual world God has made, I could have. Of course we can *imagine* a different result ensuing, given all the datum up to a certain point. But this is not because the world is not coherently and necessarily connected to itself, but rather because we are not omnisciently aware of all these connections as they truly exist in the world. Is it raining in Japan today? *May be*, we say. But this is not so. It either is or is not; thus the truth either is or is not. We do not know, so we think that in the world it could be either one. But that is merely us imagining reality in different ways. The reality itself is what it is, and our ignorance does nothing to overturn this.

"Still, how can someone be blamed for his sins if he could not do otherwise?"

I note, first, that if someone *could* do otherwise than what he does, then God's plan for the world, supposing it relied on the free acts of those who sin—acts which, for example, involved the crucifixion of Christ—could have failed to come to fruition. That is, if the sin could have failed to come about, the plan, if it depended on the sin, likewise could have failed. Secondly, I note this. If being able to do otherwise is necessary for blame, and if people are blamed for what they do, then the old notion of an all-predetermining God is incompatible with the punishment of humanity, since no blame can be laid on human beings. But I do not see why someone cannot be blameworthy if he does what he cannot help but do, supposing that what he does he does of his own consent and volition. The idea of reward and punishment does not follow upon the spontaneous ability to contingently do otherwise, but the fittingness of consequential reward and punishment, based off the intention of the agent in his moment of acting.

"Do you then admit a compatibilism between free will and determinism? If so, how is it *just* to punish someone if they cannot avoid their acts?"

To this question I pose another. If someone *could* have done other than he did, what purpose does punishment serve *then*? To correct him in the future? But, since there is no necessary connection between a cause and its effect, what reason is there to suppose that punishment *shall* correct him? You may punish one in any degree you like; his will, since it is indeterminate to the good, may as equally become better or worse. Punishment therefore may be useless. The accomplishment of its end is a mere spontaneous event, unessentially related to the punishment itself. And even if punishment did work the effect intended—which would be a matter of chance—why think that the man is any better for being corrected, seeing as, in the future, he may repeat the same faults as before, since his will is not necessarily determined by the good it now more fully apprehends?

On the other hand, the idea of an all-necessary relation among things does suppose a very different notion of punishment than one commonly espoused. It supposes that, in a good universe, punishment exists for the betterment of the one punished, for making him right, and not merely to destroy or further torment him. I grant indeed that on the old notion, punishment is irreconcilable with freedom and guilt, or at least if such a combination of infinite punishment and necessary sin existed, the universe in which the two occurred would not be the universe of an all-good and all-lovely God, but a God who required never-ending torture in order to be himself, which is no God worth believing in at all. But on the notion of punishment as correction, as a bringing into a more glorious *completion*, I see no difficulty.

If punishment is not given to correct, punishment must be a good thing simply because of the destruction and suffering of the one who undergoes it. If such is your belief, or if you can stand to believe it without being suffocatingly troubled by it, I leave you to it. I only call on you to ask yourself this: what would the heart of Jesus Christ look like, presented with the fact of a human being—made in God's image and therefore his brother or sister—being annihilated or tortured for eternity? Answer that question to your own heart as honestly as you can—as honestly as *you* can, I say, and not as honestly as some bygone thinker or some system of theology answers it—and I have no more to say. You are my brother or sister. Our hearts are close at home, even if our intellects are worlds apart. For you are honestly wrestling and searching in the most humanly-divine way possible, by opening your heart to the Son and laying the awful question before the feet of the Divine Humanity.

I believe a person is bound to the measure of his knowledge of God insofar as he answers the following question: how would the heart of Jesus view the eternal destruction of a human soul? Every person ever born is *someone's* child. There is, or has been, a God-infused love in *every* human being. Has there not pulsed through every human heart the infinitely hopeful aspiration of union with the divine love itself? For what is human love, what is human hope, but this? Hope and love do not exist on their own in the soul. They are babes sent forth from the heart of God. They draw their life, always and everywhere, from his infinitely living spring of love. For this reason, if true love and hope have ever been born in human heart, then God himself has been born there. Where such have dwelt, God has dwelt also. How therefore suppose such a tabernacle laid waste? Would it not be the greatest defeat imaginable, the greatest tragedy thinkable, to suppose that hope and love in human soul could be destroyed, or snuffed out, or ultimately forgotten? In such a soul, would not God—Immortal Life itself—die?

If God could die in human heart, how then could hope, how then could goodness, yea, how then could very love itself be eternal? How could life be greater than death? How could God be the strongest thing in existence? In a word, how could God be God?

Ears of Corn

Is there not a true potential in each soul for beatitude, for infinite love and happiness? I ask how a Christian could deny it if he believes in an omnipotent God who has made creatures to share in his own beatified life. Yet, if we love our fellow humans, how is it bearable to suppose that such a glorified potential could be lost, or fail to come to fruition? How is such a thing tolerable? How could the creation existentially tolerate its own ability to be forever lost and therefore its own power to make wickedness as strong as goodness? How can we, if we see our neighbors as ourselves, ever *accept* the fact that some souls shall *never* fulfill the purpose for which they were created; that some souls will not become one with the heart from which they came? How could almighty God justify such a situation to himself, or how could the supposition of such a being justify itself to us as a God, if the creature is eternally at enmity with its Creator?

I can well imagine being perfectly satisfied in God and all the evil in the world if I knew that the good beings who suffered it were worth enough to be necessarily destined for some higher, now unimaginable, form of consciousness and life. But how is creation endurable if, for every soul that begins to exist, it is indifferent to the divine being whether or not it is glorified? If God can pass over any particular soul, how is any soul itself inherently worth anything? How is human life anything other than a valueless collection of matter, which may or may not be collected in a certain way in the universe?

I ask, how does such a metaphysic, where a human *can* be damned, and where a God *can* tolerate that damnation, not lead to the nihilism of humanity? The good of the cosmos is the same whether that person over there reaches heaven! Can God be satisfied with his creation, or can we his children be satisfied loving his creatures, if we know that for everything that ever comes into being, everything is just as perfect if all God's creatures suffer and die or are eternally glorified? In order to accept such a thing, or even to believe it possible, one must disbelieve in the inherent value of humanity. For insofar as humanity is *necessarily* valuable, and insofar as the love and goodness in each human are *real*, humanity *cannot* be a thing indifferently cast aside. We come then to this. If human persons are inherently valuable, human persons *must* reach the full measure of their possible perfection. To suppose otherwise is to suppose there exists some maximum potential of good in a thing which God cannot or will not bring about. The more one loves all humanity, the more he sees both himself and humanity as one grand organic family, oriented towards the beatitude of God.

Was It Not Necessary?

The more one contemplates the absolute envelopment of all created being in God, the more he sees that life *must be* greater than death, and that this could never be otherwise. He who sees God as the All in All sees that, always, in every soul that comes into being, life grows ever-greater and must grow ever-greater, and that this is the will of God. To him who loves God and hopes in him, he knows that love is the greatest thing there is or even could be. He sees that no soul in God's creation could ever be finally destroyed, least of all simply for the sake of its own punishment.

Why do we need some to be damned, friends, for us to enjoy our heavenly beatitude? Is God himself not enough, nor the loved ones to whom we are united? Must we have others suffering eternally to see how good we have it, or to most fully enjoy our love? What! Is our life in God stoked by the fires of eternal death? Does suffering give life its *essential* joy? Are not love and goodness and transglorified relation strong enough to stand on their own?

To one who feels that the necessary perfection of each person hollows the world of meaning and makes of us mere puppets, I ask: shall a mother's love for her child be any less meaningful, any less intimate, any less alive, any less real because the mother cannot *but* love her child? A soul in love knows that, were it required of him, he would gladly die for his beloved. He knows that such would be a *blessed* necessity. Wherefore then is love affronted? Yea, is it not rather increased, being stronger, more determinate, more impossible to fail? Or must love somehow be *able* to fail to be meaningful or worthy of hope and life? How could that be? Who would want it to be true? I pray my love of wife and neighbor and family shall grow such as to be *unable* to be less than unbreakable. If I speak to a Christian, what would it mean to suppose that for love to be real it must therefore be capable of failure, of not being given? If you believe in the Incarnation, I ask, could Jesus Christ have failed to do the Father's will? If you believe in the Trinity, I inquire, could God himself, in his own relations of love, ever-giving, ever-receiving, ever-enfolding himself, could the triune God ever fail to love himself? Are his almighty and eternal loving relations any less lovely or grand because they are *necessary*?

Freedom is not the absence of necessity, friends. It is when the soul and the necessary laws of its being most perfectly overlap in its consciousness. Indeed, must not true and perfect freedom in action be true and perfect necessity in act, and therefore conscious bliss? Nor does this rob us of our agency. Rather, it establishes us as rational lovers of truth and goodness.

Ears of Corn

We cannot but pursue the good, as we cannot but assent to the true: for these two things, being bigger than ourselves, are thus outside our being and dominate the whole scope of our action. And thank God! To imagine that we could even possibly be drawn towards the evil *as such*, or even possibly assent to the false *as such*, is to imagine the human being an irrational enigma: a creature who finds its end in falsity and twisted oblivion. Yet such a thing, being an absurdity, could not be, or if it was, could certainly not know itself to exist; could not know itself to be capable of reasoning and loving and contemplating God; could have no notion of the "good" or "true" at all.

I would thrust my belief in the necessary connection of all things upon no one. May each believe what he will. For my own part, I know that if I am wrong, something greater shall be right and true. All I insist on is this: trust altogether in God. This simple thought is all I care to expend my energy in defending, either to myself or my neighbor. I believe it is but our stunted attempts at holding this pure and simple faith that brings the twisted turns of spirit which lead to selfishness, meanness, and despair. Such low natures are what Christ saw among his fellow men and women when, looking at the crowded throng, "he had compassion for them, because they were harassed and helpless, like sheep without a shepherd."

9

He Had Compassion

"When he saw the crowds, he had compassion for them, because they were harassed and helpless, like sheep without a shepherd."

MATTHEW 9:36

IT IS A SOURCE of great joy to know that there are many places in the records of our Lord which describe him as compassionate. In the Gospels, the root word in Greek which is often translated as *compassion* is the word *splagchnon*. It means, "to be moved in the inward parts." Such parts are defined by Strong's as "especially the nobler entrails—the heart, lungs, liver, and kidneys." Ah, friend! How refreshing to imagine—does it not send a flash of joy to think—that the very inward parts of Jesus Christ often gushed forth waves of tender feelings towards his fellow human? Let us look at that compassionate, human heart of Christ, and so learn more about the man himself.

Why did Christ come? Why else, but to kindle into roaring flame any heart who had in it even the smallest ember of the divine? Surely, if he loved all humanity, Christ would have prayed for all humanity's salvation. Surely, he would have prayed to God that every human of the race would be saved from any ill that prevented it from being a perfectly free and glorious child of God. And is not the human desire of Christ heard by God his Father?

I ask you Christians who believe in the Incarnation, could Christ ask anything of God, if he asked with true request, which God would not grant? If Christ could truly desire a thing and ask it of the Father, and if the Father could still deny Christ's pure and honest request, then is there not possible enmity between the will of the Son and the will of the Father? If there is division in the heart of Jesus and the heart of God, then God can deny himself, and there is no more hope for humanity in his all-perfect Fatherhood. For God could deny his own created human need, the Son who comes forth from his bosom.

Yet if Christ must obtain from his Father all that he asks in purest request, then all who Christ prays for—that is, all humanity, since Christ loves every human being—must be delivered from their state of sin. The point is plain. If Jesus truly desired the salvation of all, and if he truly asked God for such a thing, then such a thing must come to pass, since the working law of love that rules the heart of Christ is nothing less than the will of God, worked out in the world and manifest in the flesh.

Or did Christ not love all humans? Did he desire "justice" for those who were in sin, and therefore wish for and desire their coming condemnation, their future eternal torment? How then did Christ tell us to pray for the forgiveness of our enemies? How then do all Christians every Sunday pray for all the humans of the world? Is it with pure intention? Does "all" really mean "all"? Does the church *really* desire the salvation of everyone, or should it, if not even Christ himself did so?

And what of that church? Can the church through all time ask something of God, can it desire through all ages with burning heart the deliverance of the whole creature, and God not grant such to his bride?

I ask again. What of Christ's command for prayers to be made and acts of kindness done universally to all, even sinners? Did he then tell us to pray for the *unjust* deliverance of sinners from a coming punishment that was *perfectly just*, which they ought to suffer and which he himself desired that they suffer? Did Christ tell us to ask from the Father that which he himself did not ever truly want to occur?

Or did Christ only conditionally pray for the deliverance of humanity? That is, did he pray that the race would be saved from sin and therefore delivered from eternal torment, but only if God arbitrarily wanted them to be? Then his love was not for his fellow human as such, but for God's arbitrary will, whatever it happened to be, whether it chose to save his brother-beings or not. That God loved Peter and Paul was fortunate for Peter and

He Had Compassion

Paul! Had God, from the foundation of the world, reprobated them, Christ would have nowise wished their salvation.

I would not be mistaken. I do not say that there is anything wrong in praying that God's will be done. To align oneself with the will of the Almighty is the height of perfection and a state which we must all one day come to rest in perfectly. But to pray that God's will be done when that will is itself indifferent towards either of two opposite fates is to pray, not for a good essential, but for an indifferent unessential: an ontological insignificance, where the value of humanity is lost in the void.

God is goodness, and goodness is necessary, eternal, and true. It cannot be other than it is, or it would be other than goodness. Christ prayed for the will of God to be done in the sense that he prayed that all goodness would be done. But Goodness cannot be indifferent to opposites. Else it would not be goodness, but indifference. It cannot be as equally good for one to be damned as it is for him to be saved. If it were, why ought we want anyone to be saved? The spirit of Christ's prayer was not, "whatever your will is Father, whether it be finally good or bad for this human being which was created through me, whether it be that some of your children be tormented forever or annihilated or all brought to heaven: whatever your will is, may it be done." Rather, I believe the prayer of Jesus was "Father, I know that thou art good and cannot but be good. May thy perfect goodness, the glorification of humanity, come to pass as thou wilt. For I could not conceive a better outworking than thee if I spent a thousand ages tracing out the steps. Even my notion of "better" comes from thee and is but a shadow of thy full heart. May thy perfect will be done. May I live in that will and see it in fullness and draw life from it. I trust that thou art perfectly good; therefore I trust thee completely. I give you myself and my human brothers and sisters. Even if I cannot see how, I know thy perfect good shall fall on all."

Thus the whole prayer is not a request to change the mind of God but a prayer of praise and confidence and abandonment into the absolute necessity of God's Goodness.

The Good pulls all things, reconciles all things, corrects and transmutes and beatifies all things. It is irresistible, simply because it is itself. For that is what the Good is: the highest, most supreme ruler and puller and harmonizer of all life and thought and action. It is the one grand desired thing, the ultimate victor, the ontological triumph. Because of this, it can have no opposite.

"All this sounds very fine, but the words of Jesus himself show us that some will be lost forever."

Even if they did, how would that justify you in believing them, since to believe them you must therefore cease to believe in a good God, the God of Jesus Christ himself?

"We have the parable of the sheep and the goats. Jesus says that the Son of Man will come again and separate the good and bad once for all at the final judgment."

Whatever the coming of the Son of Man meant, Jesus said that some of his hearers would be around to witness it before their death. How then could it involve some final judgment, where God, looking at all humanity who has ever lived, once *for all* consigns some to *never-ending* punishment?

What then did Christ mean by his coming? Could he not have meant his resurrection and his consequent making of all things new? I ask, what would the resurrection of Christ usher in but the beginning of that "regeneration" of all things? [1] In his overthrow of death by dying on the cross and rising again, Jesus comes infinitely closer to the heart of every man and woman. Christ is risen, therefore has eternally sat down on his throne of life. Thus his power in creation must begin to work anew. Is he not now judge, living his full power and glory, having been made perfect by his suffering? Has he not now come, yea, is he not now coming all the time, sending his angels into the hearts of everyone through his resurrection, renewing all? You tell me Christ will come again to judge, once for all, and maybe he shall. But I say, is he not now—not always—on his throne, judging, separating sheep from goats? Are not all nations always gathered before him? What Jesus says in the parable of the sheep and goats is nothing but the same universal law of God—the one divine way with humanity—where the compassionate ever enter into the kingdom, which is life, and the selfish go ever into their own self-imposed prison, which is death and fire and the gnashing of teeth. Do not all men and women, throughout their lives, go through such a winnowing by Christ, entering into both life and death? Verily are such rewards and punishments eternal! Verily, everyone is ever-resurrected, to both a punishment and a life, the punishment itself leading and giving rise to the life, for everyone has done deeds both good and evil! To suppose otherwise would be to suppose that God made a humanity which was perfected by something other than the single law of love.

---

1. Matt 19:28

I know many of my readers will wonder what I take to be the resurrection of the dead, if I suppose that the apocalyptic words of Christ may refer to events in Jerusalem in 70 AD. If the Lord has already returned in glory and began liberating those who were asleep, what then of us who have not yet died? If the coming of the Christ—that which Paul and James and Peter and the early Christian world thought would happen *soon*, yea, very probably in their lifetime—if such a coming of Jesus is now truly past, is there no *universal* resurrection at the end of earth-time? Will Christ not once for all "come again in glory to judge the living and the dead"?

I do not wonder if my readers should ask such things, for I ask them myself. Do not angels desire to look into them? I will only say that, so long as the whole human race lives and moves and has its being in our all-beautiful God, whatever the answer to such questions, all shall be well. Surely God judges all men and women in his own time and will let none off, nor any into his kingdom, without having them pure. What is the resurrection of a mere *body* at a certain point in history, in relation to the grand truth of the universal fire of judgment, sent into the heart of human soul by Almighty Love? Is *this* really where we place our infinite hope in God—that a combination of matter we call "ours" is brought to life once again, with or without the whole human race, at some future time? Could not some have already passed from death into a greater life in God? Shall you demand that such an existence be a "bodily" one when you cannot even conceive what such a higher awareness of God's presence could be?

What we want is not a raised body simply, but an expanded form of conscious being. We want more life, more love, more relation! We want more God! Truly I hope, and by my Christian faith I believe, that a drastic transformation will occur in these regions of existence when I die. But do I not also know that Christ helps me grow in my life and love and relation *now*? Even now, Christ helps me while in this body expand my being: he helps me become greater than I am. By asking him to come into me, he makes me more, and opens my soul to existence. This is my Christianity. Such a faith can be had by the simplest heart, at any time, by simply asking Jesus to *come in,* and *open my heart.*

I do not know how it happens. I do not know how the soul makes contact with the Lord. But must I? Can I not close my eyes and think of a loved one—my wife—and, somehow, make contact with her? She may be miles away physically, but—now by my mere will and thought—becomes present in my soul. If I can do such with my wife, and thereby call up strength and love and faith in the goodness of life, why cannot I do so with Jesus Christ? If I imagine wrongly and God sets those right who try to know his Son, then God shall set me right, if my fancy leads me astray. If the whole thing is a fiction, and the contact I make is nothing but a product of my own imagination—a relative manifestation of illusory consciousness—then so be it. I shall die with the hope that it is not, and never know the difference.

Still, I would press my interpretation of the prophetic sayings of the Lord on no one. What I offer I offer only as possible, therefore able to give room for hope in some sore heart, ensnared by the letter. Do not doubt that Christ shall explain his own words in his own time. If what we think about them is not true, something better will be. For my part, however, it takes no great faith to imagine that in the providence of the Almighty, God may have permitted some vagueness in the words of Christ which could imply, or been interpreted to mean, things very different than what was literally true. Or can God create a world where genocide and betrayal and the slaughter of children occur, and not permit a man from Nazareth to be misunderstood about certain of his claims, or about his identity? Christ's words were not intended to give all men and women encyclopedic, factual truth about the future. His apocalyptic messages may have been, like his parables, used purely to spur his hearers to action, not to settle *speculatives* about the end of the world. I do not say he was mistaken—(yet if he was, would that destroy your faith in an all-beautiful God?) I do say there may be more to his words than you imagine. Perhaps you take for granted many things which, given what you grant of the nature of the perfect loveliness of God, need not be true about Jesus of Nazareth or his *own* beliefs about the future. Could he not have adopted the people's *mythos* and belief and clothed his truths in these forms, to communicated his teachings? Is such *impossible*?

I ask, would not Christ, seeing the heart of his hearers, have known just what they could and therefore ought to hear? Perhaps, given the nature of the listeners, all they could understand of God was that it was possible for him to send them away into punishment? If they were of such an understanding, would it not be good for Jesus to stir them to love their neighbor, by kindling the fear they had from their own impure notions? True, given their nature, they may not have believed that God could reconcile all. But would it not have been good of Jesus to meet them where they were, to draw them out of themselves? Even the motive of fear, as low as it is, can bring one out of darkness, if it leads to the first step of obedience. Does not the same principle apply to us? Is it impossible to believe that Christ could have talked in such a cryptic way then, when he allows even some of us now to continue believing in our own error, in our own low notions of God, and so suffer the consequences of our false images of the Divine, sprung from our weak faith?

What! Can we only trust and hope in God and love our neighbor if we believe that, necessarily, the apocalyptic words of Jesus pointed to the never-ending torture of some of humanity? In order to love God therefore we must necessarily believe that some humans are damned! God cannot be loved unless there is a universe where some souls suffer eternally! What kind of faith trusts the written words of a book, themselves perplexing and at times seeming to contradict, in place of the living and breathing Spirit of God in his heart?

Christ was a teacher of truth, and a teacher of truth exists to make his students true like himself. But the teacher often knows that, given the nature of his hearers, although he may have many things to tell them, "some things they cannot bear now."[2] At times Christ giveth milk, for we cannot receive solid food; yet among the mature there is a wisdom spoken. It is not hard to believe that Christ's words as recorded in the Bible come to all as the great Dilemma and therefore Evolution of the soul, where not even his words themselves, whatever they could seem to mean, can destroy the soul's faith in its great God. No word, no verbal utterance can press in closer to the heart than the very God who made that heart. No heart therefore can rest content in mere words alone. For its perfection it needs a perfect faith, not in something spoken, but in God himself. Why, if Christ could raise a soul to such an alpine faith, where no created thing, no spoken utterance, no possible thought or image, even if they seemed to come from Jesus himself, could shake that soul's trust in the necessary all-beauty of God—I ask, if Christ could lead his disciple to become such a soul, would Christ not have made a true Christian of that one, a true follower of himself? What human word could deter Jesus' faith in God? What possible doubt, what parable, what saying of prophet or text in holy book, what image even in his own mind, could make Jesus believe anything less than absolutely everything about his God? If Christ could lead a soul to such a trust, where the soul stood on its own legs of faith, and not some *possible* faith from another, would he not have fulfilled his purpose in ushering in the kingdom of God, by raising up an altogether strong, pure, divine child of his Father?

2. John 16:12

Christ says, "Why do you me good? No one is good but God alone."[3] The greatest teacher knows that the student exists to one day stand on the same footing as himself, so the two can enjoy the truth together. At length Jesus says, "I do not call you servants any longer, but friends."[4] Christ exists to point us to his God. He works so that he and we can be one with his Father. Are we to imagine that Christ wanted to love his fellow human—that we are to want to love our own loved ones—and that both us and Christ desire to our heart's bursting that such ones be saved and eternally glorified, yet that God the Father, who is Love itself not will the same? Where did our bursting love of spouse, of child, of friend, of pet, yea, in some noble hearts even of enemy and foe: where did such come from, if not God? Did God not put the eternal feeling into us? Did he not create in us this very desire of an infinitely outstretched human love? Are we then to think that the love in our hearts for all humanity will meet in God a love at variance with this our own, which he made? Verily, no! Love cannot be so divided. What it envelopes is one, and its pulse throughout all existence is one. Therefore there must be—there cannot but be—a final harmony of all wills and all loves at the root of all things.

There is then a divinely unbreakable umbilical cord between the created and the Creator—between the first-born Son of the Father and those later born sisters and brothers—which, by his Spirit, gives us a guarantee that, despite ourselves, God *will* set all things right. But if God will set all things right, therefore too all souls. Indeed God's whole relation to us his creatures *is* this setting right. This setting right God does, and shall continue to do, until he sees that there is no more to set right, until we cannot be righted anymore, because we are absolutely right, utterly at oneness with him, and thus fully glorified children, enjoying in blessed gladness the house of his universe forever. God shall continue his labor until all his children are brought home into closest unity with his Father-heart. For the whole human family is under the divine and omnipotent care.

I ask, how is it that Christ has perfect compassion for our race? Is it not because he, being fully human himself, saw his humanity struggling, low, and afraid, staring back at him in his fellow man and woman? Christ could not have seen man or woman, however wicked, and failed to see his own essential humanity, else he would have lacked compassion and therefore fallen short of perfect humanity. This is compassion: to *enter into* another.

3. Mark 10:18
4. John 15:15

Thus Jesus Christ, being the infinite human, and being thus infinitely compassionate for all, entered into—indeed is now entering into, and forever will be—every human ever born.

We call to this Jesus as our elder brother, the pioneer and perfecter of our faith, who showed us how to walk humbly with our God, and altogether trust and hope in him. This life of Christ, this pure and strong faith, makes us stammer with a hope unspeakable when we proclaim that, through him, "we have obtained access to this grace in which we stand; and we boast in our hope of sharing the glory of God."

10

Boasting in Our Hope

"And we boast in our hope of sharing the glory of God."
ROMANS 5:2

ST. PAUL WRITES THAT we—that is, all believers, and all those who hope in the resurrection of Christ—"boast in our hope of sharing the glory of God." Some translations render it as "rejoicing" in hope. Ah, friends! To rejoice in a hope altogether pure, to possess a trust absolutely free of suspicion! Who does not see that this is the very essence of hope and that, insofar as we fear that we shall not obtain the glory we seek, we are that much further from a pure and perfect hope?

To the degree that our hope is tainted with fear, then, to that degree, we are not hoping. No doubt hope must be sown in the soil of hardship and uncertainty. Therefore it differs from knowledge. Yet the flower which buds and gives rise to the rejoicing that the apostle here mentions ought not to be a dead thing or in the process of decay. Hope must be for the Christian a source of joy. I do not say it cannot be attended with tears. But I do say that, if it is to be pure, it—like love—must cast out all fear. How therefore can one hope in God his Maker if he believes that Maker capable of damning him forever? How therefore can one love his neighbor and hope for his salvation, if that neighbor may be tortured for eternity?

Even those who believe in a never-ending hell will tell you that they *wish* it were not true. They will tell you that they *hope* that, in the end, *all* will be saved. I do not doubt their feeling. I only ask how their hope is authentic, or how it is consistent with the other truth that they hold, namely that some souls in fact *shall* suffer forever. If what is commonly held to be divine revelation is true, then some—most?—*shall* be damned. There is no getting around the fact. But how then could one hope or wish otherwise? Can a person hope that divine revelation is wrong? Can he who holds by faith the necessary truthfulness of a proposition concerning the afterlife, at the same time think that proposition false, or even *possibly* false? If you believe divine revelation infallibly declares that some *shall be* lost, how then can you honestly pray for all? If divine revelation cannot err, then it cannot be true that your prayer for universal salvation shall be granted. How then pray for it?

"We are not to pray for the salvation of all, but only to desire that all be saved."

Why do you desire their salvation if you know that they will not be saved?

"For to desire their damnation would be wicked."

Shall we desire that which God has expressly told us shall not come to pass? Is that not disobedience, or at least idiocy? Hence the same difficulty arises. How *desire* that all be saved, if all shall certainly *not* be? I do not ask if one cannot hope and pray for and desire universal redemption. Surely one can. I ask only how this feeling is not absurd, yea, at total odds with one's faith, if he believes in eternal torment. Shall not God's will be done? Surely, you say. How then is your hope not at odds with his will, if you are his child? Thankfully your soul shall not let itself hope for the final destruction of your human brother or sister. Yet how does the tension between your hope in God and his will as you perceive it not tear asunder the communion of your soul with its God? Where can you hope, but in the will of God? Yet how can you hope in the will of God, if his will be not altogether good for all?

A person may say he hopes for the salvation of all, but *if* he does, *when* he does, he cannot also be holding to the *certain* damnation of some. His hope is (at that point) inconsistent—indeed irreconcilable—with his doctrine. For this reason most are in constant flux between what their hearts want for their fellow human and what they believe that a tradition of men teach is true. But others take a different way. They hold that, although some will be lost, and although there is no getting around the fact, still, in the end, "all will be well." In heaven they believe they shall see the final righting of all wrongs, and everything will be finally reconciled and brought to a completed harmony. There shall at last be a state of agreement wherein they shall say, "Yes, this is good," and *feel* it true.

Assuming they get to heaven themselves! How can all be well if you are not there, friend? Yes, all shall be well—for the souls who are filled to overflowing with joy infinite and unspeakable! But what of the others? They still exist. Is it well with them? If not, how therefore is it well with you, well with all? How can the universe be *all* right and good if *all* are not right and good, or if *all* shall not be, someday? You say all wrongs will be righted. What about the wrong of eternal torture felt by a being made in the image of God? If God is satisfied with such a condition, if an eternally lost soul could really be a finished product of infinite love, why have any confidence that *you* shall be among the saved? If God can bring into being that which he has no obligation to perfect, or which he is satisfied with in not perfecting, why suppose all will be well with any person, including yourself? I ask, why think God shall not be perfectly content with permitting *your* damnation?

"Because of his grace, by which I am saved."

Yet that grace need not be given to all. Why therefore think it given to you?

"Because I believe in God, and in Christ, and feel his grace in me."

Then God must be such as, to those whom he gives the grace of belief in himself and his Son, therefore they must be saved. God *does* then have some obligation, to his own gift of grace, to see to it that those to whom he makes believe he shall certainly save. Do you then say that, if one has believed, he cannot be lost? Do you say that God must honor his initial gift of grace, to bring to glory those who have at one time truly believed in his Son?

"Yes."

But you have said that God has no obligation to what he makes.

"It is a self-imposed, freely chosen obligation. Once grace is given, it cannot be revoked."

And you know this is so how?

"Because of his word."

But God is such on your theory that he is under no obligation to give us his honest word or, if he did, to keep it.

"The Bible is the word of God, and God cannot lie. Therefore what the Bible says cannot be false."

If God can create conscious, loving souls to be tormented for all eternity, what prevents him from lying? Or can he inflict endless torment, but not lie?

Note also how we have moved away from talking about God himself, now to some written word about him, handed down by human beings. Wherefore justify the unmade by the made? Does the unseen rest upon the seen, the uncreated upon the created? As if the Bible explains God such that *he* must conform to *it*! If the *Bible* says that God cannot lie, *then* God cannot lie! What! Can God not lie simply because the Bible says so? How absurd, to trust in some description of God, when the God behind the description is impossible to trust in in the first place!

To trust in God is not, and cannot be, to trust in some book about God. It is to trust in God himself, as he is in his own necessary perfection and essential loveliness. To substitute trust in God for trust in his book, however mighty and beautiful and lovely that book may be, is to trust in something infinitely less than God himself.

It is often said that no one could know a personal God unless that God freely revealed himself, and that the revelation of the Bible is therefore our only way of knowing God's relation to us. God is unknowable, such say, unless he speaks. I ask, cannot God speak in the heart? If he can speak on a page, can he not speak in a conscience? Shall God's written word be more trustworthy than the heart from which that word has come? Why believe what comes from God into our minds if his word tells us that he who speaks in our minds is incapable of hope and trust? God's word cannot have more integrity than God himself. Therefore no written word of God could ever describe a God delighting in the torment of lost souls, nor a God weak enough to justify to himself bringing them into being if he could not save them. Any revelation from God, then, must be pure enough to make trust in that being something possible, nay, necessary, else it would be useless. What good would a revelation do, what would be the point in studying it if, at the end of our inquiry, we arrive at the conclusion that the being who gave it could not be trusted, could not be hoped in? The whole enterprise would be futile!

"But we must trust in God. Else life becomes unlivable, hope impossible."

Indeed! But that comes to this: we must trust in the necessary goodness and unconditional love of God, for it is only on such basis that we can ground our hope in the first place. Otherwise what we termed hope would spring not from love, but fear, and therefore could not be strong enough to give eternal life. Even if we are mistaken, even if there is no God, or even if there is an evil God, we cannot hope in anything less than an all-loving principle that is necessarily altogether *for* us. If our hope shall live, it must cast its roots this soil of gold. Hope cannot stand on shifting ground or sinking sand. It can only lift its eyes confidently to the heavens and spread wide its wings if it believes that the giver of its life is something altogether good for it, yea, that it cannot even in principle be bad for it. The giver may be bad for it for a time, or it may appear bad for it, but hope, if it be hope, must see these ills as transitory, as bowing towards an ever-greater, more glorious beauty.

But if that which has breathed life into us, friends, is altogether for us—or if we must believe this in order to live—then it must also be altogether for everything that we love. What could be *for* us, or to say the same thing, what could *love* us, that did not also love that which we loved? Does a mother love a child who has no care for the child's loves? No doubt the child may love very low things, and no doubt the mother will want to correct the child, to redirect it to higher things. But this is only because the mother loves the child and wants what is best for it. The redirection exists, not to take away the loves of the child, but to enable the child to more fully love the very things it loves. Would not a perfect parent seek to do this in the grandest way it could, not with child loves only, but with all loves—yea, with very love itself in the heart of its child?

I ask, what is best for mankind—for all God's children—if not to love God and each other? St. John tells us, "Whoever does not love abides in death,"[1] and "Those who say, 'I love God,' and hate their brothers or sisters, are liars; for those who do not love a brother or sister whom they have seen, cannot love God whom they have not seen."[2] Can we then love God, brothers and sisters, if we do not love each other? And can we love each other if we find it *acceptable*, or if we are in any way *indifferent* to the fact that, some of us *will* be lost forever? How can one human really love another if he can justify in his heart the ultimate destruction of that other? How has his love not shrunk, wilted, yea, evaporated into unreality? If you

1. 1 John 3:14
2. 1 John 4:20

love something—not to say another person—how can you ever tolerate the utter destruction and loss of the thing you love? Ask yourself! Look your loved ones in the eyes! Can you find it acceptable that they could become to you as if they never were? Can you ever find it tolerable that that human there—that person who has laughed and cried and wanted happiness and been afraid—shall suffer in unimaginable, lonely agony, *forever*?

Who have you loved, and *really* loved, that you could bear to part with, knowing that now that that one is gone, he never shall breathe or smile or have joy again? I do not say perfect love could not be content in never beholding the beloved again. It could, in the strength of its perfection, throb unwounded by the separation, but only if it knew that the object of its love was itself happy, was fulfilled, that it neither suffered nor lacked, or if it knew that, should it suffer or lack, it was all in the end for its own glorious good. Thus love's action would still be itself and still be complete, insofar as it rested in the beatitude and good of the beloved. Yet how could this be, if the beloved was no more? How could love throb perfectly pure and healthy and without wound, if the beloved was miserable, was hopeless, yea, suffered an agony of soul darker than the void, never-endingly? What weak love is this that now calls itself love, which could ever be content with such? If such is its essence, it is not eternal, not infinite, not divine! It may cool and dwindle; it may evaporate and cease! Would that God and Jesus Christ do not love us with a love like this! Would that we do not love each other with such!

Can a person ever desire or accept his *own* ultimate destruction, his *own* eternal torture? Yet we are told to love one another as we love ourselves. To the degree that we love our neighbor as ourselves, then, we must be at war with—we must find utterly intolerable and unacceptable—that neighbor's damnation. Insofar as we resign ourselves to another's lostness, or even possible lostness, we have to that degree ceased loving her. We have ceased finding her necessarily valuable. We have ceased to declare that the destruction of love is an intolerable thing! Have we not taken the lover out of ourselves, out of our heart, and put them in a corner unseen and uncared for? There they may rot or suffer, or, for all we care, cease to be. We thus kill them in ourselves; we remove them from the organic family-unity which binds their humanity to us as siblings. We trivialize them and make them unloved by God, thus no longer images of him, no longer valuable. We *give up on them*, and so make them into *nothing*. Thus we dehumanize not only them but ourselves.

"But God says that some shall be lost. It is plain in Scripture. Do we not then *have* to accept such a thing?"

To *have* to accept the will of God! To suppose the will of the All-Perfect Love-Beautiful could be a bitter pill that we *had* to swallow! What is this other than to suppose that God is not Almighty Love? That he is not essential Goodness? That he is not altogether Father and altogether *for* us, yea, the one thing best for all that is?

"In loving God, we must love him so much that we do not care whether any of his creatures are saved or lost. For he alone ought to fulfill us such that everything else is inconsequential."

If God had never created our neighbors, it would be enough that we not love them. But God has created them. And not only that, he has created that in us which is fulfilled and finds its joy in loving them. God has created us therefore as dependent on our neighbor, as that which finds its own perfection in its loving other people. In a word, God has created not only us and our neighbor, but also the very relation that arises between the two. He has made the very bond, the very relatedness, the very essential dependence itself. There is not only *person* and *neighbor*, but *neighbor-in-person* and *person-in-neighbor*. Such realities of relation are themselves unique phenomena that must be accounted for by an all-loving God. The question is: are they to die? Or are they to be perfected by our God?

There is a space carved out in each of us specifically for all the others of our race. It is the infinite compassion in us—our Jesus Christ—the movement of each soul into its fellow soul, which thus lets us *become* all that we know and all that we love. We therefore desire and are perfected by our entering into another's singular individuality. There is a need in us for a unique satisfaction that can be attained only in our loving the entire variety of God's humanity. If there was but one human left in the cosmos, one lone individual who was its own unrepeatable spark sent flying out of the divine Fire-Heart, we would still yearn to meet, to connect with, to become one with and participate in, the existence of that one. Must there not then be a space in us, not only for this or that person, but for all people, yea, all possible people, which is filled only by our loving each?

God has made us and our neighbor one, for the two are only explicable in relation to each other. Neither is explicable in isolation. Who is my neighbor, except someone other than myself? Thus my understanding of *myself* necessarily involves the idea of some *other* that is not myself. The definition of my neighbor, then, enters into the very constitution and definition of *me*. He is that which I am related to, but not identical with. I cannot then even know myself without knowing my neighbor, nor know my neighbor without knowing myself. The two are essentially, inextricably, connected. Likewise there is no humanity without humans individuals, and there are no human individuals without humanity. Should I cease loving my neighbor, so too would I cease loving the humanity of myself that I essentially participate in—the universal humanity of absolutely everyone.

God made me to love himself in loving myself, which means at the same time in loving my neighbor. Therefore to love God, I must love both myself and my neighbor. It cannot be possible to love God *and not* my neighbor, for then I would not be loving myself, whom I must love to love God, since he loves me also. To love God then must mean to love everything relatable to myself, that is, to love everything God has made. Do you not see how the whole chain of love is linked together? If there be a break anywhere, the whole thing crumbles!

Ultimately there can be no disharmony in love. All things, from the atom to the human to the galaxy, love themselves insofar as they seek to maintain themselves. In a word, all things *like* themselves. They naturally love and desire to be what they are. Thus they behave according to their nature, and in doing so reach for and arrive at their loveliness. This self-enjoyment is part of every thing's glorious imitation of God. Likewise, since things are continually being themselves, they too, like God, are continually reproducing themselves. This conspicuously applies to humanity. By the mere fact of our being human, we therefore love humanity. Our life is a continual enjoyment and enriching of our humanity, a constant duplication and reentering into it, a playing with it, and a never-ending rediscovery of it. This is not and cannot be bad or wicked. Indeed, it would be absurd for us to hate our humanity, for that would be to hate ourselves, to deny the very purpose of our nature. It would be for a creation of God to turn in on itself and destroy itself, for it to be a thing the goal of which was to move essentially backwards, whose meaning was to unmake itself. No doubt we hate things about our current condition: our sickness, our anxiety, our troubles and cares, our hardships, our selfishness, our fears. But these hates only arise out of a deeper love of the perfection of what we have when we are fully ourselves and fully alive.

Yet, if we really do love humanity as such because we are human and therefore cannot help it—our loving ourselves being simply what it is to be ourselves—then from the fact that all people are humans, we must love all human beings; for we are essentially like them and in them all. When I look in another's eyes, do I not see, somehow, myself—something like me? How then can I be careless, unless I be careless about myself? Like all true thoughts, once this is seen, it cannot be unseen. The essential connection of all humanity has the universality of a divinely simple thought: a *truth* of existence. You and me, reader, are of the same nature. That fact alone contains a mystery deeper than human knowledge will ever exhaust. It means that you are *in* me and I am *in* you. I may not even be alive when you read this. Or I may exist thousands of miles away. Yet somehow, my spirit is now dwelling in you. Here now, even as you read my words, I am living in you and taking shape and growing. What is the glance in the eyes of a stranger, but that stranger coming, momentarily, to live in you? What is the sound of human voice, or the touch of human form, or the smell of human figure, but that very soul somehow washing into your being? All humankind, all individual people, are in you, and you are in all. We are all in one another. Thus insofar as any human is lost, and I accept that fact, I have ceased to be human. I have ceased to love myself and have cut myself off from the divine relation I have to my humanity, for I have ceased to see in the lost my own humanity standing there, reproduced, looking back at me. To desire or rejoice or be fulfilled by or accept the ultimate destruction or corruption of another person is, then, immoral, that is true. But in a deeper metaphysical sense, it is absurd, for it requires the absurdity that a nature be perfected by the willing of its own destruction.

If eternal enmity between humankind is possible, if the saved and the lost can be possibly eternally opposed, if the brother or sister across from me, who looks me in the eyes and whose common humanity dwells in my very self also, can fail to reach the only thing that makes their human life worth living, and if they can become forever tormented and miserable, how can I love anyone at all in this world? If such things are even possible, each person becomes ultimately expendable, a mere *indifferentia* that, for all that concerns me, I may have nothing more to do with! If this is reality, did love ever even exist in human soul? Did man or woman ever really feel for one another that which is stronger than death? Shall a heaven which made the loss of all my earthly loves tolerable not itself be a hell far worse than one of flames of agony? The greatest torment that could befall a soul is not the torture of fire, but the thought that all his loves—yea, and love itself as he had known it—were not real, not eternal, not the highest, most grand thing in reality, the only thing worth existing for. Even if a good man were in hell, so long as he knew that some were in heaven, so long as he knew that at least *somewhere, somehow* there were some enjoying a primal and boundlessly perfect love, he himself would not be truly lost, for love would still be aflame in his heart.

How hope in God, if the perfection of human nature is such as to rend the very fabric of humanity? How hope in love itself, if the love which knits together the human family will one day be torn asunder? How is the world tolerable—or the God who made it—if this is the way of things? Will God unmake the nature he is making? Will he, at length, cause the human heart to be unmoved by suffering, by the spoiled potential in the damned, by the destroyed friendship, the eternal enmity between brothers, sisters, family, friends, yea, children, yea, spouses, yea, lovers?

May we never believe it! If we have ever truly loved someone, it can never be false that we truly loved them. There now exists for all eternity that relation in us, that real love which links us to what or who we loved. And though the memory of such loves may fade, and though time may quiet the emotion that used to bubble and flow so freely out of our hearts, still, this does not mean that we never loved. For see how even the memory of forgotten love excites the spirit to hope in that very love's resurrection! Even if there were no God and no afterlife, the human condition would still have loved, would still have had hopes of a resurrected, glorified, and eternal love for one another. For even if the universe dies a heat death forever, it would still be true that there existed love between husband and wife, friend and lover, daughter and mother, father and son. Not even an eventual nothingness can make it that such things never were! Such is the immortality of love itself—that even if death is the end, death cannot make it so that we never loved!

Since those we love are truly in us by our mutual love in times past, there is in us that which was uniquely made by them: a footprint of their soul imprinted into ours for eternity. Thus, were I to find that I could not believe in a God or a hereafter, I would still believe in the reality of the love I have had in my heart for those I have loved. By clinging to it, I would therefore keep my loved ones alive, and bear them with me until I died myself and was no more. Even should my brain decay until I forgot it, no amount of degradation could ever destroy the fact that *I truly loved and was loved*. It can then never be false that those I loved were truly one with me in the deepest part of my being. Such a thing *was*, therefore is true, *forever*.

Let us then flame the fires of our loves and love all as truly as we can, where we can. And let us believe that what was begun in us will one day be perfected, even if we cannot at present see how. Our hope ought to lead to rejoicing, friends! Hope should not lead to death, but life. Because of this, and because we crave eternal life, our hope must be infinite. It must rest on a foundation greater—necessarily greater—than anything we can conceive. But the greater must exist in the upper direction, not the lower. It must take up our loves and glorify them; not negate and forget them. I ask, is that person there—hold him in your heart, reader, or look at her with your bodily eye—I ask, is that person there, who you are looking at or thinking of, is that human being worth saving? If you say that he may have been once, but at any rate is not now, I wonder how you could call yourself a Christian and think that Christ died for *you*.

If anyone was *ever* worth saving or *ever* worth Christ dying for, then, in a universe made by an omnipotent and all-good God, such a one must be saved. But then all must be saved. The Father *must* see the travail of his soul and be satisfied. Therefore we believe—we cannot but believe, if we are to believe and hope at all—in one who *shall* "reconcile to himself all things, whether on earth or in heaven, by making peace."

11

To Reconcile All Things

"Through him God was pleased to reconcile to himself all things, whether on earth or in heaven, by making peace through the blood of his cross."

COLOSSIANS 1:20

IS NOT THE ONE purpose of the universe, the one goal towards which it moves, to become the divinely idealized and perfected form of itself? Insofar then as anything in the world is not fully reconciled to God, it has not yet attained the end for which it was made.

To suppose God made a thing only to suffer and die, or to suppose he made it to reach its end as a decayed and stunted form of what it could have been, what is this but to say that God did not make the thing for its own sake, for its own goodness? For wherein lies the thing's *telos*, its ordering, its perfection? If a thing finds its end, it must find its goodness and completion. Thus, to the degree that it has not yet reached its end, it is to that degree short of goodness and incomplete. How then could eternal torment or annihilation ever be a creature's end in God's good universe? Such a state, being the very essence of an incompletion, could therefore only be a creature's interim—never its finality. If this were not so, then the lost creature could never have been directed to, could never had a potential for, eternal life. For how could omnipotent God intend a creature's glorification, and that glorification fail, without God losing his creative omnipotence? Unless you think that God *intends* any creature's ultimate destruction? But to suppose that there exist such creatures—to suppose, moreover, that some of them are human beings—is to say that they were never rational beings moved by truth and love to begin with. If a thing has ever loved or has ever known truth, that thing must be made in the image of God. Therefore it can only find its home in God. It could never have been made *in order to be* destroyed. Since God is eternal, indestructible life, that which is made in his image must find its home in this life. It can then never be ultimately lost.

Nothing can love, nothing can grasp truth, nothing can consciously yearn for happiness, unless it has in it a spark of the Divine, unless it is made as an image of God. If the thing is a human, it is the Christ in him—the Divine Humanity—that makes it so. If it is not, it is the divine form whereby the creature relates to its Maker, who loved it into being as a manifestation of himself. But if, then, all humans have Christ in them in some measure, then all humans are bound to a full reconciliation with Christ's Father. This must be so. Were it not, Christ would not be the Word made *human* flesh. Some human would exist outside the uniting bond of the universal humanity of Jesus. Since Christ is human, he is connected to all humanity. Since he is divine, he is assured of his victory. In Christ, the divine reconciles the human. This did not begin simply when Christ came into the world. From the beginning of the beginning, when the universe was first breathed into being by the Father through the humanity of his Son, God predestined to create for himself a glorified human race.

What could ever happen, what conceivable pulse of human heart, what act of will, what desire, what motive, what possible movement of human brain could ever come about, that was not pre-contained in that first creative breath of the Father, whereby he made the world through Christ? If God made the world through a principle of humanity, then all that could ever exist from humanity, must already be accounted for. It must already be enfolded in the creative relation between creature and Creator. Any potency whatever, whether in soul or body or spirit or brain, is a potency already rooted in God's creative act, and therefore in God himself. Yet God himself is essential and Almighty Love. What then could come about that could thwart his will of redemption? What power of human nature—the power itself having its scope from God's hand to begin with—could usurp the end towards which God was pleased to predestine that power to move? To say God could fail to reach the goal towards which he works and the glorification of each created soul, what is this but to say that God did not create the soul: that it did not come from an all-loving Creator: that its home is not altogether in him? Does created soul stand eternally—necessarily—against Creator as uncreated?

Once you say that God created the soul, not only must God be directing it towards some end, but he must also infallibly achieve his end. Else there would be something in the soul unintended, unaccounted for, uncreated by God. Therefore I ask again: could God, Almighty Love, create souls destined for *final* destruction? Verily, no. What good—what purpose—would these souls be made for? To enhance the glory of the saved? But the saved, considered in themselves, were already predestined for glory. How therefore could they have been lost? How therefore can they appreciate that which they never could have failed to attain, unless you go back and undo the predestining of God? Yet if God's predestination cannot fail, then a predestined soul cannot but be saved. How then could an elect soul rejoice in its salvation compared to a lost soul, since it was not possible for it to be lost in the first place? Or was it possible, before the world was made, for God to elect any soul to either heaven or hell indifferently?

To suppose that God elects certain souls for life and others for damnation is to suppose that souls in themselves, independent of their creative relation to God, stand as already existing—though valueless—pieces, which God then arbitrarily gives a certain share of his goodness to. To this one he gives this good, to that one that; he predestines this one for heaven and passes over that one for hell.

But, in fact, such a thing cannot be. There can be no *independent* existence of the soul in itself, undirected to some end, unmade by God, where God stands back from it and *then* decides to grant it more or less blessing. Once the soul is there, it is there, already like the God from which it came, already fully related to him, already with a capacity for love, already bearing the image of the divine, yea, already made through the humanity of Christ. There is no "human soul" considered in the abstract, pre-creatively in the mind of God, where God stands back and chooses to elect it or pass it by. To posit the creaturely reality at all is to simultaneously posit its nature—therefore its value and end. Away with the absurd idea of the whole damnable mass of humanity eternally confronting God *first*, and *afterwards*, God choosing what to do with it! Is the life of God divided? Can any creature exist at all without that also entailing that God is already creating that creature? It cannot be. Where would the "considered soul"—that one which God looks at and *then* decides to give saving grace to—come from?

Ears of Corn

Does God simply *find* himself with this valueless but existing entity, this necessarily existing potential, which he can then arbitrarily craft as a vessel of mercy or destruction? Without him already creating it, how could the thing in question even exist—much less deserve punishment—so to allow God to have *mercy* upon it? Who has made it if God can go on to give it grace? If it does not even exist, how then does it naturally deserve wrath?

We are not our own principle of existence, true. Therefore we are not necessarily life itself. Thus our coming into being is from God, who is life. But it does not follow from this that we naturally deserve wrath or torment. Even if we *do not* deserve to come to be—a proposition which, if God necessarily deems us valuable in his own essential being, may be debated—even if, I say, we do not naturally deserve to exist, it would not follow that we therefore are deserving of eternal destruction. To say we are unworthy of eternal life, even to affirm that it comes to us of pure grace, is not to affirm that we are otherwise worthy of eternal torment or annihilation. The negation of the first does not entail the affirmation of the second.

Do you say that the damnation of the lost is necessary so the saved may more glory in their deliverance? I ask, how can heavenly bliss feed off such a low thing as mere *deliverance* from suffering? Is eternal life not strong enough to find its joy in life *as such*? How faithless, how unimaginative, how lifeless to think that our beatitude in God will be perfected by our own thankfulness that it was our fellow human, rather than ourselves, who lost his pearl of great price! Can I not enjoy my own treasures of the kingdom unless someone else is deprived of his? How much like a nursery of snatching, selfish children heaven will be! What then would be the difference in the essence of heaven and the essence of hell? See how backwards this system is—how many absurdities it leads to! In such a metaphysic of confusion, how refreshingly clear is the gospel message: the good of one is the good of *all*.

I submit that that entire notion of grace and predestination, that whole relation between God and humanity, as proposed by the scheme of election and reprobation, is meaningless and false. It imagines both God and humanity as eternally opposed existences, which *begin* to meet after having been *naturally* alienated. It imagines God as the necessary good and mankind as the necessary evil, and therefore fails to see the essential relation that is in each to the other. God decides to *change* his relation to creation, from a possible parent to an actual one—yet to a human race which already exists to be loved! To all the could-be elect that God passes by, their being is still wholly unaccounted for! Where did they come from, if God can look at them and pass them by? Behold the contradiction: before God creates, creatures exist in his sight necessarily, whose very existence is contingent! Before he creates, God knows that which cannot but be known unless he first creates it! The whole error in the scheme is that it fails to see that the faces of God and man are not eternally opposed, but forever looking in each other's eyes.

"To be at all, is a gift of God. God is under no obligation to give more being to some than to others. He is perfectly within his rights to grant some heaven and to let others live in lower planes of being."

What is meant by "lower planes of being"?

"Perhaps hell. God is justified in displaying a variety of modes of being. Some modes approach more to himself—these are the heavenly souls—and some recede further away and approach closer to non-being—these are the damned."

Why must diversity involve hierarchy? Or rather, why cannot hierarchy be displayed in a variety of kind, and diversity involve a horizontal display of mode, each mode itself possessing, uniquely, as much being—therefore as much a reflection of God?

As Dante says

> *As for the leaves, that in the garden bloom,*
> *My love for them is great, as is the good*
> *Dealt by th' eternal hand, that tends them all.*[1]

In such a diversity infinite, the poet sees an infinity of leaves, all bearing their own non-competitive splendor. In the next world, why need there exist any subordination such that the subordination itself brings about endless pain to one of the very things which was created to show forth God's splendor? Aquinas himself says, when discussing the innocence in the garden, "The cause of inequality could be on the part of God; *not indeed that he would punish some and reward others, but that he would exalt some above others*; so that the beauty of order would the more shine forth among men. Inequality might also arise on the part of nature as above described, *without any defect of nature*" (emphasis mine).[2]

Evidently, inequality can exist and display beauty *without* eternal punishment, pain, or even defect of nature. But if the end can exist—diversity

---

1. https://www.bartleby.com/20/326.html.
2. http://www.newadvent.org/summa/1096.htm.

Ears of Corn

of being—without the untoward consequences of eternal ruin, torment, and loss, why do they?

"Eternal punishment exists to show forth the justice of God."

Do you mean by "justice," "divine punishment for sin"?

"Yes. For that is what justice is, the punishing of sin."

But not surely the *mere* punishment of sin, for many Christians are punished in this life and are delivered from that punishment in the next. Something more, then, must be required—namely, the eternal, the *never-ending* punishment of sin—else God's justice could be perfectly displayed without it. Therefore I ask, must never-ending punishment exist in order to show forth the nature of God?

"Yes, justice is an aspect of the eternal God, and justice requires everlasting punishment to be perfectly displayed. Therefore it must be manifest in his creation."

Then for God to be God he needs the everlastingness of evil. His righteousness is met with an equally opposite and essential force of wickedness. Goodness does not of its essence overcome evil, but stands opposed and irreconciled to it, eternally.

In fact, punishment—and therefore justice—is an incomplete notion, an abstraction among human relations, existing in the minds of men and women only to serve some higher end. Its whole purpose is to turn the thing in which it is working towards something better. Thus "justice" as it is conceived as mere punishment for the sake of pain, can nowise exist in the perfect universe of God. Is divine justice achieved—is it truly *served*—in the damned? If not, then justice is not displayed after all, for justice just is an act of appeasement, of setting right. Justice is a thing complete in itself; it does not admit of degrees. If it is met, it is met entirely, or not at all. That is just the meaning of the word. Therefore insofar as justice fails to be met, we have not justice, but *injustice*, and justice has not been served; the thing in question has not been set right. How then say that justice is shown in the damned if it is not truly and finally served, if all is not righted? The whole scheme, predicated on displaying the essential justice of God, fails to display the very necessity which it calls for!

On the other hand, if justice is fully served in the damned, why do they continue to be punished? If we have appeasement and setting right, we have finality. If we have justice, we have completion, else punishment is always striving towards, but never attaining, the end for which it works. Thus if justice can be met, punishment can in principle be fully paid, and continual suffering may cease. Why then is pain eternal? Do you say that the damned continue to sin and thus *accrue* more debt? The point remains: concerning the damned, either there is a point at which justice is paid, or there is not. If there is, then, what happens after that point could not itself be a result of previous punishment, for punishment has already been paid. Thus the damned would be, for a moment at least, free and set right. They would be given justice and God's justice would be displayed. If you say that they cannot possibly be free or set right, and that they are determined and solidified into their wickedness, I ask why. If it is because of previous sin, then you presuppose some lingering punishment that still exists in their nature which inclines their will towards this wickedness. In which case, once again, punishment was never really paid in the first place—and never will be, for all eternity, if they are to remain eternally wicked.

If there is no point at which justice is met in the damned, then their being in hell does not display God's perfect justice. At most it would be but a defective justice: therefore injustice. For the ideal justice to which "imperfect" justice approximates would be something aimed at but never achieved. Again, wherefore does justice admit of degree? Insofar as something falls short of the divine justice, the thing is unjust, for justice is the perfect instance of what ought to be present. How then is it coherent to talk about the divine justice justifying the existence of hell, since hell itself falls short of displaying perfect justice?

I ask those who believe in eternal torment, who cite God's justice as the reason why it exists: do you believe that Christ's sacrifice fully appeased the *justice* of God? And if you do, why suppose God need create a populated hell in order to demonstrate his justice? Was God's justice not perfectly displayed on the cross? And is not divine justice perfectly *satisfied* in the just—yea, the *righteous*—who are saved? Through Christ's saving work, those in heaven perfectly appease and therefore display the justice of God, do they not? Yet if the saved can show the justice of God perfectly, then God's justice need not require eternally tortured souls for it to be displayed. Especially since, in the damned, justice is not fully met, which is why they continue to suffer.

In fact, is it not true that God's justice is *more* displayed in the saved? If it is not, then suffering souls show forth God's justice more than the righteous who are clothed in the work of Christ. Christ's work must then be weaker than the torment of the wicked. Yet how could the work of the Divine Man be weaker than any other human force, any outworking or action or willed choice by creature? Shall the righteousness of Christ shine less brightly than the unrighteousness of the wicked?

Or should we think that divine justice is equally displayed in both the saved and lost? But then how could it be better to be saved than lost? If the goodness in the saved is their relation to God, and if they as equally display the same attribute of God as the lost, then how can there be any distinction between the two? What would be the difference, metaphysically speaking, between saved and lost, if their *good*—their participation in God—was identical?

Yet if the saved display God's justice more, then not only does God not show his love in the lost as greatly as in the saved, neither does he show his justice as greatly. The saved show forth *both* God's justice and his love *more*. Why then does hell exist? Why did God create the lost, if his justice was more poorly shown in them by their own suffering than it would be by their perfection and beatitude? Did God create a hell that need not exist in order to display a justice that could more brightly shine?

How, brothers and sister, do the damned bear the image of God? How does his Spirit shine through their ever-hateful faces? How is such a soul's creation justified, who despises forever the one absolute good in all existence? How does Christ's work touch the soul in hell? Does it touch it at all? And why not, if Christ died for all? How could a human soul exist, utterly unconnected to Jesus Christ? If the work of our Lord does touch it, how then can Christ not be victorious? Does his work meet some obstacle it cannot overcome? God forbid! Else love is not the mightiest force in existence. How then can the victory of Jesus not be complete? Is not the death of Christ the justice of all humanity? Is Jesus's work not the almighty work of the God-man, therefore impossible to be defeated; impossible to be improved upon?

I ask the believer in eternal damnation, is there a destination of the universe *too* terrible for God to bring about? I ask, *could* God create a universe in which *all* souls were lost? And if he could not, why couldn't he? What part of your belief prevents such a thing? Surely, you say, God could not create universe x. But where are you drawing your standard? If you do not believe that God must be good to what he makes—that is, that he must do all he can to perfect it—how can you claim that God cannot make a universe in which all are lost? If God has no obligations towards what he makes, why suppose he need save *anything* he creates? Why is he not capable of creating souls come into being already in a state of torment, which then lasts forever? After all, since we know so little about creation, perhaps he has done so throughout the numberless galaxies which we can see but never journey to! Is God capable of creating souls who think that some go to heaven and some to hell, but in the end, sending all to hell anyway, even those who died with a clear conscience? If not, why not? You think God can pass myriads of uncreated though necessarily thirsting souls by, consigning them to a torment the likes of which the greatest suffering on earth is but a shadow, yet you want to give a reason why such a God cannot bring to pass such things as I have speculated? Is not hell itself the very definition of the worst thing a *creatively omnipotent* mind can imagine? And would that not mean therefore that of necessity, whatever universe of horror man may think up, the created *reality* is greater still?

Do you not see how any answer you give as to why the God cannot do such things—even to attempt an answer—presupposes some *necessary* good in God which entails an essential obligation—that is, an essential *Fatherhood* and therefore *concern*—towards his creation? And it is no mere concern only, but an infinite one—of the very intensity and perfection as that whereby God is God! God is invested in creation to the same degree that he is God himself: that is, infinitely. Or can God do a thing partly; can there be lack in his infinite? If so, then the will of God can be greater than it is! He can be more infinite; more himself! Away with the thought! Surely it is no sin to believe that our God gives no gift simply to take it away again, but only to bring forth more riches to the creature itself! Surely it is no wickedness to believe, nor any wrong faith to hope, that our God is loving enough to give the gift of himself to all, and that he is strong enough to ensure that he will be cherished by all!

"God must show his image in the creation. There is nothing else that the universe could reflect but God himself. Therefore he must perfect the whole, but not necessarily each part."

Is not every rational creature its own universe? Is not every man and women, yea, every conscious being, its own infinite and universal center of feeling and concern? From the moment we have the vaguest sense of self, however feebly we can articulate it, we become one more created universe of God. Where is the "I" that I call myself? It is here, at the center of all, of everything I perceive. It is its own universe; its own whole. Every conscious being infinitely encompasses the *all* around it, and thereby holds—and *is*—an infinite world. Each soul then is a living, breathing universe of God, containing within itself all its own times and places and meanings and loves.

Ears of Corn

It has its own unique universal relation to everything else, to its all. Each soul has its own *forward* and *backward*, its own *this is how I see things*. And this relation is no less important or real than the universe-relation of any other soul. Is God bound to perfect the one common outer universe that we all inhabit, the universe of matter and rocks and trees, but not the inner universe of each soul that lives in it? Has not the same God made the outside world *and* the inside? What indeed would the perfection of the outside universe be but the perfection of the inner universe of the souls that inhabit it? How therefore could God be bound to perfect the one and not the other? If a damned universe of material things is too terrible to bring about, how can a damned universe of spiritual things be brought about?

When comparing the worth of souls—of inner universes, of images of God—how can one be worth *more* than another? Are they some economic commodity, some material good that can be weighed and bartered? How then justify the final loss and corruption of a single one? In so doing do you not overturn the whole principle used to justify the part suffering endlessly for the good of the whole? How would it not be the same as to suppose that God made the whole outer universe to fail, since each part is its own universe, its own whole? If things are required to fail, why suppose they are required to *ultimately* fail? Why cannot each fail in its turn, only to use its failure to augment its own beauty, in the same way that individual failures in the universe themselves augment the beauty of the universe as a whole?

I ask, where is the limit of creaturely suffering drawn? And how, if there is such a limit, is it not reached by the never-ending suffering of even one creature? Is it not rather that, in God's good creation, it is only a certain *kind* of suffering that can be justified—a suffering which gives rise to a good *in the sufferer himself*? Whether or not God suffers, he directs human suffering to himself and perfects it. This he did in Jesus Christ, which was his work. Thus all human suffering, it being human only insofar as it partakes of the eternally human Son through whom God made the world, must also partake of the perfection of the Son's suffering. Since the Son is one with the Father, all that is one with the Son must be one with the Father. But all human suffering is one with the Son, else there is some humanity estranged and alienated from the all-humanity of Christ. All human suffering, then, is one with God in the same way Christ's suffering is, which means that all human suffering will one day be raised to a new life. How God justified pain, friends, was by bearing it in his Son. But his Son not only bore it: he conquered it and rose, higher than before. The only suffering that could ever exist in the universe of the Father, which he made through his Son, is a suffering that rises from the dead into eternal life.

Let us return to the beginning. When God creates, he brings some thing into being for some purpose. But purpose, as such, is good. What is made therefore must be directed towards good and find its end in good—that is, in God. The beginning and the end of the creature is the same. Thus every being ever created by God must needs find its end and home in him. This is just what it means to be created. It cannot be that God creates things *in order* to be objects of eternal torture or destruction. For such an ordering is no *real* ordering, no real end, no real relation to its source, *no real creation by God*. Who would call a rational creature's eternal torment or destruction any kind of "perfection" of that creature? And if someone would, what difference would there be in the state of damnation—it being the perfection of a man— and eternal joy?

If our words have any meaning, to experience or be directed towards either final annihilation or everlasting torment is for something to fall short of goodness, to fail to attain its end and perfection—therefore not to reach the purpose for which God made it, which is the purpose living and working in the thing itself. Each thing that exists has an essential God-created purpose which drives its action and life. Thus it has an end necessarily good for it. This just *is* its good. Yet to be tormented forever or utterly destroyed—what is this but to fall short of goodness to the greatest degree? What conceivable state of existence *is* a failure if not that of a thinking, feeling, loving being, who necessarily desires happiness and who is necessarily restless until he attains it, who in fact fails to attain it and is *never able to attain it for all eternity*? And to imagine that the creature *knows* this—that it knows beyond doubt that it will never reach its end, but live on, forever, constantly aware of this fact, the greatest loss conceivable, the greatest torment thinkable! What *is* a failure of God, if not this? Was the thing not made by him for beatitude? How horrible the thought! Is there anything more terrible to imagine, or any other universe we would want to be delivered from? How unthinkable, to exist in a state of never-ending starvation—to need and want good, but never to be able find it! To go on staring into nothingness, to be pressed upon all sides by an unbearable and empty meaninglessness, to have pain unspeakable bearing down on one forever! And to *know* that you shall never be delivered from this! God, in the name of Jesus Christ, save us from this, the very thought of which throws the soul into a blackest dismay beyond words!

Is it better to wish for the annihilation of such creatures rather than their continual suffering? But how? The creature was *created* for happiness. Did it not then have a capacity for it? What then would it say, how then would it feel, when confronted with its cessation? The moment before it was destroyed, when its eternal judgment of death was pronounced, would the creature assent to the will of God? Would it thus affirm goodness, being, life, joy, love, and selfless gift? If it would not, how is its annihilation not a defeat? What does destroying the creature do but *silence* it? Surely no victory is won! The destruction of that which has in it the image of God and is therefore capable of eternal blessedness, can never be a triumph. Only good where evil was is victory!

I say that the movement away from God can never be infinite, else an evil act would be as strong, as full of meaning and being, as a good. And just because of this, no wicked choice, however great, can ever bring about the *total* destruction of the chooser. The creature, even in rejecting God, is still operating out of some principle of good; it is still reaching towards some goodness. Its action, its movement, its willing: these are inescapably fueled by the good from the sheer nature of the creature *acting-as-existing*. It is for this reason that an *utterly* evil act, like an *utterly* evil consequence, is an impossibility. Otherwise, evil could somehow bring about the *utter* unmaking of good. So long as there is evil in the good creature, the good creature must keep growing towards its own liberation. Layers of its self-deception must be continually peeled back until it has become fully good, and so fully itself. And just because the creature must keep doing this, it can never ultimately negate itself. The chooser exists for the sake of his perfection and growth. That is the reason that he is. His perfection and growth, then, are the same thing as his being created by God. Since this is so, nothing in the chooser, nor any power that he has, could even *possibly* foil the end for which he is made. Else God made an absurdity—a thing which had its perfection in the possibility of undoing itself.

The capacity for suffering and loss therefore cannot be infinite in the creature, for only the good is infinite. Any *hunger* in the creature for happiness, must exist because God has purposefully made *a hungry creature*. Can we believe that a good God would make such a being knowing that it could be filled, while also knowing that it will—or even *could*—starve forever? I ask, brothers and sisters, is it possible for God to do such a thing and we still call him "good" for any reason other than sheer terror that we may suffer such a fate ourselves? If this image of God cannot be reconciled with goodness itself, then God's creative act cannot entail such a state of affairs, even as a possibility, for God would then be creating for a reason antithetical to the only intelligible reason we have to believe he created in the first place: to pour out goodness on what he makes, and so have his creature grow into himself, never-endingly.

I said above "whether or not God suffers." But surely, the God who is closer to our being than our own consciousness of self, suffers. He does not sit aloft, high and distant, taking into himself singularly the suffering of all his creatures, forming thereby a unified "visionary" experience. He does not see things "all at once" on his tower of eternity. There is no such separation between him and each creature to allow the mass of creatures to dilute or otherwise distort his knowledge—or rather his *understanding*—of them. God suffers in the very individual creatures themselves who suffer. Their suffering is his suffering, his experience, his life. God does not always suffer, for each creature is on its destined path of bliss, where neither the creature nor the God in it suffer any more. And yet God does always suffer, in the myriads of suffering beings who have not yet reached their full flower of perfection. The one who cannot believe, or cannot understand how God suffers, cannot do so because his God exists "out there" "in himself" away from his creatures—standing, perhaps, on some mountain top of eternity, looking down at them. But such a God cannot be, at least cannot be the real God, the God in each creature, the God being born and coming alive in each consciousness, the God that each heart is saturated by and cries to and rests in, when it seeks him. It is strange—yea it is incomprehensible, yet still impossible to deny—that the God hidden from us, the God we are searching for all our life, sometimes most strongly when we are least conscious of it, is all the while closer to us than any of the things that we have and therefore do not feel the lack of. When the soul thinks "God"—what is this, but God in the soul, thinking himself, giving birth to and therefore creating a consciousness that is looking for him? Is not this the very work of God: to begin to be in a newly created way, so as to grow into a distinct form of love, an eternal energy of conscious bliss? Where else does God exist, what else is he, other than this never ending coming to be of himself, in and through all these creaturely forms? The human self-consciousness that knows itself as an offspring of God—what is this, but God himself, beginning to know himself anew? God in humanity is humanity ever seeking, ever coming into itself through him—humanity, the God sundered from himself, now finding himself, now uniting to himself, now perfecting himself! When I say

Ears of Corn

"I"—what is this, but God saying I through, by, from, with me? God is thus speaking to God, and my consciousness, although no less my own, is also God's, in this unique way. "Where is God?" a child may ask. Would that the theologians said, "within the heart of each person"! Rather than pointing to the mountain top of eternity, would that they pointed to the chest of each individual! He is not "out there"! He is "in here"! The *out there* of nature no doubt shows us God, but it is only *out there* because it has a little bit of *in here* already in it! Each soul has its God—who is the same God in each—that is closer than any outward relation, closer than the relation even to itself, to whom that soul speaks—the Inescapable Presence—which suffers when the soul suffers, and rejoices when the soul rejoices. This God—this Presence—echoes as a reflex the conscious existence, it mirrors the need, it partakes in the joy of, that live organism which stands as a lone nerve of energy in what it calls "the world." In a word, this God is to the soul whatever the soul needs it to be; else it would not be its God! God is the soul of the soul. Because of this, the soul's one duty, the one thing that will bring it bliss, is to gift the God in it with its own happiness, by becoming the greatest and truest and most lovely thing it can be; for only then can the suffering God in it become the radiantly blissful God it ought to be! The two—soul and God, parent and child—are eternally, inescapable related! Therefore they must save each other; they must be all they can be to each other! Such a God—the infinitely individual God, the God born in each creaturely soul, and existing no where other than in such souls—is the only God worth believing in; the only God who can be a God; the only God close enough to his creatures to be their actual salvation!

If the thing does not exist—a God of love in me, in everyone, yea in all things—then it ought to; therefore I will create it, by believing it.

And yet, we can rise a little above the God born in each creature, to the unborn God who reigns eternal: the Uncreated—the Perfect Will, the Perfect Thought. If our God cannot suffer—and must he be able to suffer in order to love us, that is, to give us himself; to perfect our life and happiness? *Must* God suffer to pull us into his own joy - which is Joy itself, Fullness eternal and essential? May it not be that only an infinite Freedom, only an all-embracing *Yes* to all existence, *could* save us? - I say, if God himself, in his perfect will and thought and being cannot suffer, it is only because he wills so fully and sees so truly the utter union and blossoming and perfection of all that he makes. Where knowledge is lacking, suffering may ensue, in uncertainty in achieving one's end. Where strength is wanting, suffering may be present, in impotence to attain one's desires. But what if knowledge is unmistaking; if will is almighty? Where would be room for fear, for doubt, for frustration? All would-be obstacles would be immediately assimilated into perfect responsive action, and any ill present would be seen at once for what it was, and therefore what it could not remain being forever – what it must of necessity give rise to. Would not there be, in an infinite and perfect Thought and Will, an infinite and perfect enjoyment of existence? If God does not suffer, it is because he wills without hindrance the absolute beatitude of all his creation, and knows without doubt that they attain it. It is because he knows that He is the perfect God to all that he is God to; that he must be this; that this one fact is enough for an eternity of life, both human and divine. Ah, friends! Far from an impassible God being careless of his creatures—a carelessness which the imagination can easily attach to either a God who suffers or one who does not—the God who does not suffer exists in intensest satisfaction because he *does* perfect all his creatures; because he *will* have all his children raised into an ineffable consciousness of life and relation with him!

Suppose, then, we cannot maintain both the goodness and loveliness of God and the eternal destruction or torment of some creatures. Suppose that, after thinking about it as honestly as we can, we cannot see how both things can be true. Which belief should we lose? Friends, if we must choose which doctrine is more essential to Christianity, the absolute loveliness and goodness of God, or the eternal loss or suffering of human beings, surely it is not difficult to believe that the former, rather than the latter, is more essential to our faith. If our all-beautiful God cannot be himself unless we necessarily believe in a doctrine of eternal torture, and if Christianity has at its core the idea of eternal suffering more than it does the supremacy of love and goodness, then neither our God nor the Christian faith can save us. They doom us to a life of fear and anguish, where we beg a deity that is unmoved by our cries for a salvation that he neither cares nor has to give.

What dominates in such a religion of darkness, falsely called by some *Christian*, is the dreaded truth that, at the heart of all reality, the principles of separation, hatred, pain, and defeat are as true as the principles of life. What we thought best—that is, love strong, eternal, and pure—in the end gives way to a looming law of careless death, finality, and grief. At the very most, the darkness is on equal footing with the light. Both exist co-equally, therefore both must needs be eternal! Precious victory that, which does not assert the *necessary* supremacy of the good, the *necessary* sovereignty of love!

What a joy it is, friends, to know that, while Christianity is necessarily committed to God's goodness, it is not so committed to the final lostness of souls! What an encouragement to know that in our day and age more light is being shed on the fact that many of the earliest followers of Christ and his apostles believed in the reconciliation of all things! Read the words of that far-seeing man, Gregory of Nyssa, whose heart beat strong with the blood of our perfect God, and whose voice rang radiant before the darkness of Augustine. He teaches thus in his commentary on the Psalms: "By which God shows that neither is sin from eternity nor will it last to eternity. Wickedness being thus destroyed, and its imprint being left in none, all shall be fashioned after Christ, and in all that one character shall shine, which originally was imprinted on our nature."[3]

And likewise, in teaching students of the faith, that great man of the East says, in the twenty-sixth chapter of his catechism:

> In like manner, when, after long periods of time, the evil of our nature, which now is mixed up with it and has grown with its growth, has been expelled, and when there has been a restoration of those who are now lying in Sin to their primal state, a harmony of thanksgiving will arise from all creation, as well from those who in the process of the purgation have suffered chastisement, as from those who needed not any purgation at all. These and the like benefits the great mystery of the Divine incarnation bestows. For in those points in which he was mingled with humanity, passing as he did through all the accidents proper to human nature, such as birth, rearing, growing up, and advancing even to the taste of death, he accomplished all the results before mentioned, freeing both man from evil, and healing even the introducer of evil himself. For the chastisement, however painful, of moral disease is a healing of its weakness.[4]

I cannot believe that such an idea—the final perfection of each individual—was a belief unknown or uncommon in the days of the early church, or held for the first time by Gregory. For is not the final victory of God's love through Christ what the apostle declares? Does Paul not go out of his way to say that *all things*, yea, *things in heaven, and things on earth* shall be

---

3. https://www.tentmaker.org/biographies/nyssa.htm.
4. http://www.newadvent.org/fathers/2908.htm.

reconciled through the work of Jesus? What grander scope can be given to his words which the phrase *things in heaven and things on earth* does not capture?

Yet how would all things be reconciled, dear brother, if the damned be not one will with Christ? How are the annihilated reconciled, dear sister, if in their last moment they hate beyond words both Christ and their God? No. The principle upon which the reconciliation of the whole cosmos rests is *peace*. A peace brought about by the death of Christ: a death which all things must pass through and, in their infinitely variable modes, participate in, and thus be perfected by. Any God worth believing in is one who *shall* reconcile all to himself: therefore all human loves; therefore every possible love that ever bubbled up into heart or brain. All our hopes and dreams and loves and infinitely more shall be resurrected and glorified, friends! We can believe nothing less, or we perish.

Yet, until we reach this all-encompassing and all-perfecting reality of faith, and in order to enlarge our hearts so that we can most fully enter into it, we must heed the words of Christ and "keep awake."

12

Keep Awake

"And what I say to you I say to all: Keep awake."
MARK 13:37

DOES IT EVER AMAZE you, friend, that this thing—life—*is*?

I sometimes think that I could die from the mere fact of my vision. That I can *see*! What is it? That I can feel *love* pulse through my soul! That I can even wish for more *life*, more *belief*, more *being*! Ah, *desire*! Ah, *hope*! What wonders are these? What is a smell, a sound, the seeing of a thing? What is the intensity of odor, the harmony of music? What is the vibrance of color, the tasting of sweetness? What is the waking life of a child, a new-formed soul, a sprouting consciousness enfleshed in matter, looking out through deepest eyes, those portals to the inner world of infinitude?

That I could meet another *being* like myself (what is a *being*?) who also thinks and feels and loves is incredible, is it not? There is another *I* who knows itself as such. How is it not the wildest thing that thought could think? A husband beholds his wife's smiling face, and that very face and gladness are now one with himself. How is this? The very happiness of his wife now plays itself inside him. The husband has *become* the wife: her spirit and happiness, rolled out in material forms and conscious feelings, are now indistinguishably mingled with his own, and he can no longer tell where he ends and she begins. Where is now his wife's joy? Is it not in them both? Therefore are they not both one? Who can comprehend this? What is the mingling of loving souls? Two souls in love make love, and so produce a child. Their very love blends together such that a new *person*, a unique combination of the two, comes to be. Love therefore mingles with very love itself, and so produces new love. What is this? Who can understand it?

Even now, in reading these words, somehow my spirit—my self-love, my me *within* me—is coming into and communing with your *you*. My inside world is now becoming yours. Our bodies may never meet, but that is no matter. The spirit is higher than the body, and can transverse distances infinite and times set apart. There is much talk in philosophy these days of "counterfactuals of freedom." I ask, what is the counterfactual of a person but the spirit of that person working in another's mind, therefore transcending time and place? The person may be long dead, yet, when we think of him, we *know* him, do we not? Must the person himself not therefore be more than the physical body he had for whatever time he lived in it? When he was alive he did not *then* say to my soul many of the things he *now* says to it when I read him or think of him. Jesus Christ never spoke to me with his physical lips, nor did Gregory of Nyssa, nor George MacDonald, nor John AT Robinson. Yet I hear all their voices in me. Must their spirits not then be communing with mine? Must they not reach out and mix with me, across matter, time, and space? Must they not, somehow, be *here*, within me, *alive*?

In knowing, as in loving, as in feeling, two become one. How warmly, incomprehensibly secret! See how the simplest phenomenon silences the tongues of the mightiest metaphysicians! With what wonders we have felt, who can hope too little in what the Almighty Life has in store for us—what modes of union, what joyful play we will have with our kindred spirits—when we shall reach the house of the Father!

Yet in order to get home, we must keep awake.

To be awake we must not walk sleepily through life. We must realize that, in every thinkable situation, in every possible space of matter or mind, form or feeling, we exist altogether because of an incomprehensible, all-beautiful God. The one sitting in heaviest spiritual numbness; the brain in most profound confusion; the lover in deepest grief; the soul eaten by greatest anxiety: what do such hearts need but to know that they exist by the heart of an all-perfect, all-tender God? Ah, friend! The one blessed fact in all existence is the will of the all-beautiful God be done. To know this—to hold it in the deepest folds of thy heart always, whether in times of trial or joy—is to begin to be awake.

To be awake is to live and breathe every moment in the living and breathing truth that surrounds thy being. It is not to be concerned with *proving* anything, but with *gathering* everything. Oh soul! All thy God lies about thee. Gather him in, bring him close to the fireside of thy heart, so he can warm thee! To be awake is to desire to talk, explore, question, and approach; it is to feast on truth, love, beauty and peace, to assimilate all such into thyself. It is to come not with arguments, not with demonstrations. To demonstrate is to destroy. To appreciate is to enrich. To keep awake is to come in eager hope and sympathy. It is to seek creative union and new meaning, both with thy fellow human brother or sister and with thy world around thee. It is to let the feelings of all enter you, and to so feel their feelings also. It is not to attack or wound, unless to heal; and it is never to negate or dismiss. To be awake is to reason *with*, not *against*. What dost thou gain when thou reason against? Dost thou seek to prove a thing to *thyself*? Why then reason against thy *neighbor*? Dost thou seek to prove it to thy *neighbor*? But why, if thy neighbor be not seeking of his own heart in the first place? Yet if seeking of his own heart, why not reason *with*?

Why do we strive to keep awake? What is the feeling of awakeness *for*? Verily this: love. That is, growth and saturation and satisfaction in love, in loving, and in being lovely and full and true. All things exist for the blossoming of their loves. This is why Christ came: to help us live; therefore make us like him—therefore make us perfect in love. His coming was his giving himself, and himself is his own keeping awake. Did Christ not show us that the one goal of our being is to perfect our humanity in its own self, its own love, in all its bravery and honesty and depth and beauty? Love as it is in God himself—love infinite, love simple and pure, Love Essential—is beyond anything we will ever comprehend. It comes to us in fragmented forms: now joy, now laughter, now sorrow, now anger. It comes to us, in a word, in our humanity. It comes to us in Christ.

Do not let the existence of sorrow make you doubt the primacy of love. How could sorrow negate love? Every emotion blooms into itself from the seed of love, for love is the driving energy of all human feeling. Does one weep for loss? It is because he loves, not loss, but that which is lost. Somehow the distance between him and the lost causes a love which shows itself in tears. Were it not for love—yea, love unspeakable—no tears would come. To wish to abolish tears from the world would be to wish that it made no difference whether we lost what we loved. But then how could we love, if our not having what we love made no difference to us? Since we love—since we are even able to love—therefore we cannot be indifferent. That which we love must already be in us, as part of us, affecting our being inescapably. We cry, then, not because there is some evil in us, but because there is so much good breaking forth upon us that we wish to tears that we could unite ourselves yet closer to it. Sorrow is but the heart's cry for more of what it believes with all its strength is truly lovely. Sorrow could not be, were it not rooted in love itself. Therefore sorrow could never usurp its supremacy.

The purpose of our being is to love with our deepest, purest, truest, strongest, most tender humanity. This is to reach our maturity in the full measure of the stature of Christ. Friends, we must come to see—we must come to *feel* and *know*—that this is so, and that this *must* be the way of things. Ah, what can mere words hope to convey? They stagger along after thought and feeling, and the brain fumbles to understand itself by forming them. The soul is ever-trying to present to itself some intelligible account of what it feels and what it is, but it cannot. For what truly occurs in feeling and in loving and in being, is infinite. To one who has never loved, what could words tell him? You may as well describe color to a blind man. If a man has loved, then words convey no new, unfelt reality. They merely recall to the palate of his mind that which he has already tasted. Words therefore are but the misty leftover of feeling: ever-trying, and ever-failing, to bring back that which the soul once enjoyed.

God—like love—is too big to prove. What is a proof but simply the going back over some conscious experience? To prove a thing, the thing must already be present in the presentation of the proof, or else we could never get to it. "If x, then y"; "x, therefore, y." But then we are just reproducing an experience. We must already be familiar with x, otherwise we could not proceed. One could not understand a syllogism that started "If ?"—for it would mean nothing. A proof therefore is simply the mind playing with its own past consciousness, rearranging it, trying to harmonize it, attempting to pin it down to some definable, trying to squeeze from it some sort of *must be*. You can never get to a thing that you have never conceived, never yet had any notion of. First you must have the thing. And *that thing* you do not prove, you simply find yourself with.

"You do not think that we can prove the existence of God!"

Ears of Corn

What good would it be to know beyond doubt that God existed, if it did not make us better men and women? The question of proof is either irrelevant, or a thing of speculative entertainment.

"But at least we would be satisfied in knowing for sure that God *was*!"

Satisfied? I say that we cannot know God in the way that we wish—our wishes being manifested by our attempts to prove his existence to irresistible satisfaction—until we see him face to face. But then we shall need no more proof. Syllogistic proof therefore is something which, even if it was possible, would be by nature unsatisfactory: a paltry substitute for living communion with the living God!

The apostle says that in this life we know things "dimly."[1] The literal reading in the Greek is "in a riddle." I ask, do you think you shall ever get free of the riddle that saturates your being—the riddle of existence itself? The assertion of any fact, however trivial, carries with it every question conceivable: therefore an infinity. Why then seek a certainty that is at odds with obscurity, since it is plain that this is impossible? Even supposing you answered all your questions to your satisfaction, how could you know that there was not some devastating argument, some unthought counter-point, which would overthrow your answers?

The question of "how" can be multiplied endlessly. For what is "how" wanting but some common mechanism of explanation? Yet the mechanism, for all our common experience of it, is no less mysterious than the question that gives rise to it. Every mechanism can itself be inquired about, can be interrogated for an explanation. Must we not eventually come to a thing necessarily impenetrable, because not mechanistic at all—but simply itself? All our questions terminate in the unanswerable question of how God is God. "How does God know the future?" we ask. "By creating it," we say. "But how does he create it?" we rejoin. "By being himself." "But how does he be himself?" Who can answer such a question? Who can even comprehend if it is comprehensible? Shall any soul that ever lives be able to tell *how God is God*?

Such is the human dialectic: the unknown God drives humanity to the creature, and the creature drives humanity to the unknown God. To comprehend that one does not comprehend the infinite God, and yet know that he is still seen in everything like a familiar face—that he is still heard in all things like a primeval echo—is to begin to know God with more than the mere intellect alone. It is only by giving up our effort to grasp the ineffable

---

1. 1 Cor 13:12

mystery of God—it is only by ceasing to close our fist around him—that his secret flower begins to bloom. Only thus can we enter into the garden of the Lord; only thus can we attain our full inheritance as children of God. The key therefore is not to abolish the riddle of life, but to become such that we find ourselves at home in it. We must, friends, allow ourselves to rest in our own uncertainty, in the mystery of our being. Is it truly a defeat of intellect and will if we trust that that mystery is a perfect, all-relating God? Surely there is something bigger than our questions. Something must envelope them and contain them, else we could not think them, could not even ask them at all. Why cannot this thing be an all-perfect principle of love? If a thing *may be*—why, what other reason do we need to believe than that it *is*? And if we cannot believe it, we can surely hope for it, can we not?

We can—we shall! I will do so now. Join with me!

Are you afraid because the truth may be too terrible, because God himself may be unknown—even unknowable? What is unknown may be either feared or hoped for. Why then fear? If God is unknown, he *may be* worthy of our hope, may even infinitely surpass it. But if he is worthy of fear, he shall be as terrible when he comes anyway. What then could fear do but add to the terror that will already come? We must have enough courage to have faith!

Look at us, Christian brother, Christian sister! We who believe in Jesus Christ, and who believe that he taught us by his action, that the grand principle of Existence ought to be looked at as a loving Parent, we act as if our God would be angry at us for being unsure, or silly, or farting, or making love. We act as if God would be mad at us for being *human*! Oh friends, if you suffer from such low notions of God, join thy heart with mine in banishing them forever. Let us trust our Maker more than that. Let us trust our humanity which came from him—a humanity which Jesus shared to the full—more than all imperfect and half-true metaphysics. I say, let us let God be God, and let us trust him and his universe enough to think that he is not offended at us when we let our humanity be itself and enjoy it for what it is and for what he made it—yea, and what he is continually making it, forever more. Let us, friends, once and for all, cast off the fear of an unloving, selfish deity, and put in its place a God of perfect, absolute, tender-giving love. Our God is our great deliverer, our ever-present, our all-relating. He is the endless Mystery into which we walk; the all encompassing Myth in which we consciously choose to participate. He is the Great Warm Secret in everything—that which is in all and is therefore infinitely concerned with all. Let us approach him through Christ—the eternal humanity—and always call to him as our Great Parent. Let us hope all we can of him, and love all he puts in our way with him.

We must begin living and hoping now, friends! We must begin trusting, begin loving, begin growing in Christ's confidence in his Father and our deliverance. We must do this now: this very day, this very moment! Let us never turn back to the shell of the god we left behind. We are told that all things work together for good for those who love God. How many think this means that God chooses who to love and who to hate—and how many are wrong! It is the loving *of God*, the trusting *in* him as all good, that *makes* all things work for good. Therefore, beloved, we believe *in* God. We believe in God because we must believe that Almighty Love is the greatest thing there is, yea, the greatest thing there can be. If it is not true that at the heart of existence there is a necessary and eternal principle of profoundest all-relating love, it is a mistake I shall die believing. Everyone must decide what possible mistake he is willing to die for, and, consequently, what possible mistake he is willing to live for. For myself, it shall be a Perfect God, and a universe created through a principle of perfected and eternally pure humanity, born in my heart when I came into being, now struggling to become fully alive.

I have such hope for us friends, such hope. Verily life is good now—but still there is death. But after death, more life.

www.ingramcontent.com/pod-product-compliance
Lightning Source LLC
Chambersburg PA
CBHW051108160426
43193CB00010B/1362